Life After Windows

INEZ RIBUSTELLO

Published by Redwood Publishing, LLC
Orange County, California
www.redwooddigitalpublishing.com

Printed in the United States of America
First Printing, 2021

ISBN 978-1-956470-07-9 (paperback)
ISBN 978-1-956470-08-6 (ebook)

Library of Congress Cataloguing Number: 2021917791

CONTENTS

Dedicated to Sonia Ortiz, the wonderful human who operated our service elevator and rode me up and down the 107 floors of One World Trade Center at least 107 times. You will never be forgotten, my beautiful friend.

To Stephen, you truly meant it when you said I had a never-ending amount of mulligans. Thank you for being my definition of constant, and for letting me be me even when it means difficulty and criticism will follow. You didn't sign up for this, but you stayed, and that is the greatest gift I have ever been given.

To little Stephen, my fun-maker and laughter-giver. You have shared your entire life with my never-ending list of to dos—thank you for taking the backseat more times than you deserve. To paraphrase from our favorite Young Sheldon: there are five billion people on this planet, and you're the perfect son for me. What are the odds of that?

To Cynthia, the one who came on the 12th of September and brought with you healing and more happiness than I knew was possible. Watching you grow up and learning to navigate this beautiful life gives me unimaginable joy and hope. Thank you for your fearlessness in shielding me from those out there that aren't my fans—I am in awe of all your incredible superpowers.

PREFACE

O nce upon a time, I lived in New York City, directed America's largest beverage program, and drank wine every day and every night. It was a wonderful life—one I continue to think about but know I'll never live again.

It was surreal, actually: lunching at Restaurant Daniel with wine stars Jean Arnold and Ed Lauber, drinking mead served by Paul Grieco at Gramercy Tavern, going to the Hog Pit for beer and barbecue with Jeremy Seysses of Domaine Dujac. How do you convey the absolute grandeur of these events? My mother called me a hedonist. My friends marveled at my good fortune. It really was the most amazing time of my life.

But as we all know, nothing lasts forever. My time in Manhattan ended with 9/11, and I came back to Tarboro, North Carolina, my hometown of ten thousand people, where the only wine people really enjoyed was the pink stuff from the tap. Please don't be offended by this comment! That pink stuff was what you'd find in my parents' refrigerator my entire college career.

People probably believed my wine ambitions would fall by the wayside once the real wine world was so far away. Out of sight, out of mind. Not for sale, not for sipping. Far from it! The pull of this work is something only people in the wine and food business understand. All of my loyal friends who were sommeliers, restaurateurs, distributors, and the like remained true to their word and true to our friendship. They're all only a phone call or an email away, and each time I visit them in the city, they're ready to greet me with open arms and wide smiles.

People often forget the value of relationships. People often take smiles, compliments, and handshakes for granted, not recognizing that when they're genuine, these gestures speak volumes. This work isn't always about wine, lest we forget. It's about being true to yourself and true to your friends.

I no longer live in New York or run a large, fancy beverage program. No, instead, I live in the town where I grew up, run a microbrewery, and try to raise two children I adore. And I try very hard to be a good wife.

It isn't glamorous, and I will probably never be a millionaire, but I've learned the value of relationships, and I've learned that you can make anything happen as long as you love what you're doing and love who you're with.

This book tells the story of how I learned those all-important lessons.

A Note on Heartbreak and Laughter

Yes, it is true that time will lessen the pain of heartbreak, but you have to be able to live through the heartbreak without the pain devouring you.

My entire life that I remember, I have tried to combat heartbreak and pain with joy and laughter—mainly laughter. This book is no different than my life. While I'll speak of heartbreak, I will also try to include just as many stories of deep belly laughter so that the pain feels more bearable. It's a coping mechanism I taught myself, and while it doesn't ever take the pain away entirely, it helps me shift away from the feelings of hopelessness, sorrow, and deep depression that can often be debilitating. The world can be so much so often, and while it is vital we recognize the darkness, acknowledging the light too is the only way I am able to move forward. So, as I share these personal stories of heartbreak, I also share personal stories of wild ridiculousness to let laughter seep into the places your heart will allow and, hopefully, give your spirit a small pep talk, whispering to your soul: "If we don't laugh, we will die." At least, that's what my heart coach has told me for forty-five years.

PROLOGUE

Once upon a time, there was a little girl named Inie. She lived on a quiet, pretty street called North Howard Circle. Everyone thought the child was happy because she always smiled and laughed and told funny stories.

But really, she was very sad. Her parents were divorced, and she felt the loss of not having her mother live with her.

Everyone around her told her not to be sad, and so she trained herself to always be happy—or try to. She did this by always being busy.

Then one day—the eleventh day of September 2001—a great tragedy struck Inie's country, Inie's adopted city, and Inie's beloved workplace. As she watched the building where she had spent the last three years working collapse on the television screen, Inie knew her work and her friends in New York were never coming back.

Little did she know, that was just the beginning of the story.

CHAPTER ONE

Cooking: A Summer Fling Turns into a Love Affair

I fell in love with cooking in the summer of 1996.

As a college student majoring in broadcast journalism at the University of North Carolina at Chapel Hill, I spent that summer interning at the United States Information Agency in Washington, DC. It was the summer after my sophomore year, and my father had arranged for me to live with one of his cousins and her family in the capital. Instead of charging rent, my cousin asked me to cook for her, her husband, and her young daughter.

This cousin and her husband were important, sophisticated intellectuals. People who knew things. I was a small-town girl who was very happy to be a Delta Delta Delta at

UNC-Chapel Hill. My dreams were to get married, give birth to babies, and have lots of friends.

When Cousin Patsy asked me if I wanted to go to the Georgian Embassy for tea, I exclaimed, "Why in the world does Georgia have its own embassy?!" Her husband, Joel Klein (yes, the Joel Klein who ended up being the Chancellor of the New York City Department of Education), wasn't sure if I really took college classes. Social life was my number one priority, and besides believing in fun, I also believed in being nice.

But despite all these differences, it was through making dinner for Patsy and Joel that I discovered I really enjoyed cooking. I loved following recipes. I loved cutting vegetables. I loved taking ingredients and making them into something that tasted delicious.

It was a lonely summer: I interned during the day and cooked at night. But the cooking became a kind of friendship, thanks to the pan and the wooden spoon that I talked to like imaginary friends.

When I got back to Tarboro at the end of the summer, I told my dad I wanted to drop out of UNC and go to culinary school. The old Inie wouldn't even have known the word "culinary," but sophisticated Cousin Patsy had educated me in the world of food and explained that there were famous chefs in New York and that cooking was a noble profession provided you excelled at it.

No pressure, Patsy—you know, just *excel*.

When I told my dad about the plans I was forming, he shot them down immediately and told me what was what: I *would* be going back to UNC in the fall, and then if I was really serious about culinary school, I would find a job in a professional kitchen the following summer to see if it was a career path I really wanted to pursue.

Good old Dad. He always knew the right thing to do.

So, summer of 1997, I worked in the best kitchen in Tarboro: Stack's Steakhouse, a small, cozy restaurant with seventies décor, located on old 64 heading to Rocky Mount. It was the ultimate fine dining in the twin counties, and in addition to having spreadable cheddar on each and every table, they also served wine—Chablis, to be precise. Chablis from the box, served by the one and only Pearl, a woman who knew the order of every single wealthy, white customer who came into the restaurant.

The chef's name was Tom, and he was, in fact, a culinary graduate who had somehow found his way to Tarboro to cook professionally for the select number of people who could afford the prices Stack's charged. I'm fairly certain Tom was less than thrilled he had to take on some young, overprivileged sorority girl whose parents patronized his restaurant, but he allowed me to come into his kitchen and stage.

Because I was reliable and timely (not talented, mind you), he also used me for other things, like picking his youngest son up from the recreation center and retrieving his dry cleaning. Anxious to please—and to get a good letter of recommendation for culinary school—I happily did whatever he asked. I also stayed silent and never started any drama when Pearl and Rudolf Knight, the man who helped Tom with caterings, cursed and heckled Tom behind his back.

I was just a young, naive, excited child, loving the restaurant business with every ounce of my being. I didn't care about friends that summer because I had made new friends, and while not one of them was my age, nor did we have anything in common outside of our employment at Stack's, they were the only people I wanted to be with.

And so, after that magical summer of immersing myself in restaurant culture, I moved back to Chapel Hill for my senior year, and before I even finished unpacking, I found a job as a bartender at a dive bar on Franklin Street.

CHAPTER TWO

Wine: Another Love Affair Begins

After working at Stack's that summer, my dad had given me the go-ahead to apply to cooking school, provided I graduate from UNC.

However, I had been bitten by the bug, and school was so not a part of my vision that working at Hector's Down Under was the only thing that energized me my fall semester. It wasn't a restaurant; it was a fast-paced dive bar with Aristocrat liquor and all bottled beer—no wine, mind you. On Saturday nights after home games, we packed people in to the point where I'm sure we were violating a million fire codes.

We had a bouncer who checked IDs, but not carefully, and my sorority sisters and my boyfriend's fraternity brothers loved nothing more than to come in and watch me sling beer and mix shitty drinks behind the bar.

The job provided cash for going out on the nights when I wasn't working, and because I was only taking electives, I didn't have trouble keeping my grades in check and keeping an active social life.

My boyfriend lived with four other guys in a house in Carrboro, and I spent most nights there, driving my brown 1982 Dodge Ram up and down Franklin Street at least twice every day. One of my boyfriend's roommates was a busboy at the cafe at Fearrington House, a five-diamond property in Pittsboro that was easily the fanciest restaurant and hotel in North Carolina. My Aunt Cynthia, who loves all things fine, would speak of Fearrington with the same regard she used for Lady Di.

When the roommate said he could probably get me a job there too, I said, "Peace out!" to Hector's Down Under and started working Tuesday and Wednesday nights behind the village bar, making espressos, lattes, and old-fashioneds, and pouring the nicest wine I had ever seen (i.e., wine poured out of a bottle, not a box).

This was also the first time I heard the word "sommelier," and Fearrington House actually had one on the property—a female sommelier, to be precise. Her name was Paige, and she was a spritely, young, pixie-haired blonde who commanded all the respect when she spoke.

I was offered the opportunity to attend her weekly wine tastings, where I learned when tasting wines, one spits and never swallows. It was a whole new world, and I hung on to every single word Paige said, yearning for more information in any way, shape, or form.

At about this time, three girls and I traveled to Charleston for the Martin Luther King Jr. Day holiday weekend. We stayed with one of the girls' sisters, who was enrolled at the College of Charleston, and since we all loved food equally, we had planned to eat at Magnolias, the premier fine-dining restaurant in Charleston.

The four of us, dressed to the nines with a reservation for heaven's sake (in fact: this was probably the first time *any* of us had even eaten at a restaurant that took reservations!), marched into the beautiful dining room that Saturday night in January and, once the waiter had greeted us, promptly told him that we would love a nice bottle of Shar-dawn-nayyyyyy.

He must have seen us coming a good ten miles away and immediately brought back a chilled bottle of Chateau Ste. Michelle Chardonnay from Columbia Valley, Washington State, 1995.

I'm not sure if it was because we were all in Charleston together for the first time or because we'd gone to Victoria's Secret earlier that afternoon and everything had been on sale, but for whatever reason, we all agreed that it was the very best bottle of wine we had ever drunk in our entire lives. The. Very. Best. Wine. Ever.

We sipped slowly, making that $35 bottle last the entire meal between our thirsty table of four. Of course, we split the check four ways (as all sorority girls always do, to the chagrin of the server) and made our way to Wet Willie's, where we got housed on nasty, sweet frozen drinks with names like "Call a Cab."

When we made it back to Chapel Hill that chilly Monday afternoon, the first thing I did was jump in my Dodge Ram and drive to the Harris Teeter in Carrboro to see if I could find the wine we had enjoyed at Magnolias. And there it was, on the middle shelf, the same label staring directly at me.

The first thing I noticed was that it was less than half the amount we had paid at the restaurant.

Score!

I used the fancy wine chiller at Harris Teeter that was filled with ice-cold water and stuck the bottle of wine in it for the prescribed amount of time. Shaking with excitement, I drove to my boyfriend's house in Carrboro right down the road to get that bottle opened as fast as I could and recreate the magic I had enjoyed two nights earlier.

And just like that, I started my never-ending journey into the complex world of wine.

The second thing I noticed was that it didn't taste the same as the bottle I had drunk less than forty-eight hours prior, nor did it give me the same delight.

Days later that week, I discovered that this particular bottle was a different vintage: It was from the 1996 harvest.

Later in life, I discovered why the bottle tasted differently at a much-anticipated meal out with four girls living life to the fullest than it did in a rental house in Carrboro with no one around but me in a pair of sweatpants and a long-sleeved T-shirt.

Wine revelations numbers one and two: Wine changes with the year (just like people do), and wine changes with its setting—just like people do.

CHAPTER THREE

Peter Kump's to Best Cellars to Windows on the World

I n July 1998, I moved to Manhattan to attend Peter Kump's New York Cooking School.

The boyfriend had already been hired to work at Lazard Frères, a small mergers and acquisitions firm in Manhattan, so it only made sense that my cooking school be located there as well.

My dad, stepmom, siblings, and I drove into Manhattan on Easter weekend in March to visit the cooking school, where I interviewed and saw the setup. I knew immediately that this was where I needed to be, and we signed papers that Monday to secure my spot for July's start date.

At that time, I had nothing else worked out—meaning, no place to live. Still, I was determined to figure out living arrangements once I got back to Chapel Hill, and I was able to do just that by finding three girls from the Delta Delta Delta house and one from East Carolina University, all of us looking for an adventure, excitement, anything that would open up a whole new world of experience.

My dad and another roommate's dad signed their lives away (if you hear my dad tell it) on a two-bedroom apartment on the twenty-fifth floor of New Gotham, a brand-new apartment building in Hell's Kitchen, on 43rd Street between 10th and 11th Avenues.

Thanks to my conservative southern upbringing, I had not given myself permission to move in with my banker boyfriend, so instead, my dad paid for an address that was just that: an address, not a place I slept. Not that there was any room in the apartment for me to sleep anyway. A whopping 1100 square feet, we had one set of bunk beds in the smaller of the two bedrooms and another set with an additional twin in the barely larger bedroom —beds, bodies and shoes covered every inch of space in that brand new apartment with a perfect view of the World Trade Centers..

From almost the minute I arrived in the city, my entire being changed. I was drawn to New York with the strongest magnetism, in love with it like the biggest love you can imagine, and I was over-the-moon happy to be there. No homesickness, no regrets, nothing but a crazy, deep desire for my new home.

It was a life-changer, and almost immediately, my romantic relationship with the banker boy took a hard turn. I wanted to do everything, and he wanted to work. He explained to me over and over about his job, how stressful it was, how hard he had to work, and how I needed to be there for him when he got home at three in the morning. I resisted and argued and downright raged against his disciplined nature, but I stayed true, writhing and twisting in this emotional straitjacket.

Meanwhile, I was studying at Peter Kump's New York Cooking School on 92nd Street between 1st and 2nd Avenues, about a thirty-minute subway commute from my Hell's Kitchen apartment. But before I even learned about mirepoix, I found a part-time job at a wine shop called Best Cellars, on Lexington between 85th and 86th, right where I got off the subway each morning.

It happened like this: I would leave my apartment every weekday morning and walk to Port Authority, where I would take the Shuttle to Grand Central Station. From there, I had two options: I could get on the 4 or 5 express train and shoot up to 86th, where I would walk the almost six blocks to school, or I could take the local 6 train, stop at 96th Street and walk the four blocks down. I switched it up depending on the day of the week until I realized it was much quicker to just take the express train to 86th. And it's a good thing I did, since now every afternoon, I would walk by a beautiful wine store.

Completely intrigued, I walked into the shop one day to find a young, cool-looking guy pouring tastes of wine into small plastic cups for shoppers to enjoy as they browsed. Best Cellars' decor was super sleek, clean, modern, and edgy. The wines were organized into groups, such as bubbly, fruity, jammy, oaky, and sweet. One bottle of each wine stood upright with a description underneath, while the backup bottles lay on their sides in little illuminated caves. As I walked through the store, sipping my sample, I noticed that not one wine in the store cost more than $10—shocking, surprising, and totally awesome. I read almost every shelf-talker before settling on a bottle of wine to take home that evening. It was the Terrazzo white from Lazio, Italy, and it cost $8.

This same scene played out after school for the next three days until I was approached by the assistant manager, Mollie Battenhouse. A fellow southerner from Atlanta, Georgia, Mollie also attended culinary school: the Culinary Institute of America in Hyde Park, New York. Because I was the only student who wore their houndstooth pants and stark white chef's jacket to and from school—inviting many strange looks on the train and on the street—Mollie knew immediately that I was in culinary school.

She was intrigued by my daily visitations to the store, when I would sip and taste every wine I could, and read each and every shelf-talker, looking ever so dorky in my chef's getup. When she approached me that day, I had no earthly idea my life was about to change in the most unimaginable way.

Her exact words were, "You'd save a ton of money if you just got a job here."

"Is that an offer?" I said.

If you inspected my life for moments of change, Mollie's proposition would be a crucial one. I had no idea at the time, but Mollie would be the person who redirected my culinary dreams into wine aspirations.

Even today, I rarely ponder ideas, knowing immediately whether or not I want to pursue whatever offer is on the table. Within a second of Mollie offering me a job, I happily accepted.

And so it went. I left Peter Kump's every weekday afternoon at 5 p.m. and walked to Best Cellars to clock in at 5:15. My main job was to stand at the door greeting customers and pour two-ounce samples of whatever wine we had chosen that day so that anyone who was interested could have a little "toot" while they shopped. "Toot" being what my Nana would call a drink she enjoyed in the afternoon, though of course, Nana wasn't speaking of wine—she was referring to her delicious gin and water.

Anyway . . . back to my day job.

My culinary class of nine consisted of only one male: a young gentleman from Puerto Rico named Anthony. My bestie was Janice, an older African American woman from Harlem. Besides Sharon, a Jewish girl from New Jersey and also the youngest in the class, there was Helen from Alabama who was married to a bigwig in the city; Lora, a PR person; Elaine, another socialite type; Alexandra, an eastern European immigrant; and Joanie, a really sweet older lady from Utah.

Chef Michael, an extremely quiet and calm older man, instructed the nine of us from July until October. I will never know if he liked us or hated us—I only saw his expression change once over the course of the entire four months when I naively compared one of our dishes to frozen food. We were making chicken pot pies with a homemade crust, tournéed vegetables, strained chicken stock, and béchamel. "Horrified" does not do justice to his expression when I told him our chicken pot pie tasted just as good as Stouffer's.

Still, culinary school was amazing. It was four months of intense training on technique, the mother sauces, baking, and wine. I found myself studying like I had never studied before, and I was very focused on making sure I took every opportunity given to me. Finally, I had found what I loved—and at the ripe old age of twenty-two. And the wine store gig was even better than culinary school. I had never been so happy going to school and work in my entire life.

First half of the day: food.

Second half: wine.

Both avenues made me a popular roommate and a popular girlfriend. At school, we prepared a different dish every single day, and every single day there was an abundance of leftovers that I was allowed to take home to share with my four roommates. And, of course, the discount I received on any bottle of wine I purchased wasn't too shabby either.

I worked hard at both careers, with no idea how I would find a full-time job while doing either or both.

Then, on a Wednesday morning in late August, I sat faithfully reading the *New York Times* "Dining Out" section on the 5 train. Peter Kump's had encouraged us to stay up to date on restaurant reviews, so I bought a *New York Times* every single Wednesday and read "Dining Out" from cover to cover. This week, I was thrilled to see a front-page feature on a young woman named Andrea Immer, Master Sommelier and Beverage Director at Windows on the World at the top of One World Trade Center.

Here was an article focused on a career in wine! And not just any type of career: a big-time career. *And* she was a woman. I was so giddy reading on the subway that morning that I could barely focus at school that day or at work that evening. All I wanted to do was speak to Andrea Immer, and I was determined to find five minutes during a workday to call her.

The following day, I arranged to get to Best Cellars at 5:30, and after school, I went to a payphone on the Upper East Side and called the main number at Windows on the World.

"May I please speak to Andrea Immer?" I asked the reservationist.

"Yes, I will transfer you to her office now," replied the kind and cheerful voice.

And, what do you know, Andrea answered.

She fucking answered.

I stammered and stuttered, but I finally got out my name and my desire to come work for her. Andrea was kind yet stern.

"Do not leave your wine job," she told me. "Working in wine in any capacity is better than not. While I don't have anything for you at Windows right now, fax me your résumé, and we will keep you in mind when something arises."

Disappointed yet hopeful, when I got to Best Cellars, I shared the news of my phone call with Mollie and asked her if I could use the Best Cellars fax machine to fax Andrea my résumé. Mollie, who had become not only a mentor but also a kind of older sister, agreed to let me bring my résumé the following afternoon and use the business fax machine.

Of course, sharing this information with Mollie also let her know I was actively pursuing a career in wine, and so, shortly afterward, I was asked to interview with Best Cellars for an assistant manager position.

I loved the manager, Krista McCorkle, and the other assistant manager, Peter, and of course Mollie, but I knew I wanted more access to the world of wine. By this point, I had taken several wine classes at school and started reading every wine article in the *New York Times*, so I had just enough knowledge to be dangerous. And I never stopped thinking about Andrea, the Windows on the World wine cellar, and the Master Sommelier Program.

Months passed, and I quit my first kitchen internship at the trendy Moomba to opt for a much less stressful day job at the Bento Box in the basement of the Takashimaya Department Store, under Chef Ellen Greaves. The Bento Box was only open for lunch, which worked perfectly as I would arrive to work at 8 a.m. to prep and then work service, leaving around 3:30 and heading over to Best Cellars to work evenings.

At this time, my only income was Best Cellars, so I kicked into overdrive to make sure I was bringing in moolah for my nights out. The Bento Box was also open on Saturdays, and I was paid on those days since my stage only consisted of thirty-five hours. Meanwhile, my over-the-top generous father was still paying my rent along with other amenities.

I loved Ellen, the executive chef at the Bento Box, and her small staff, but the more I worked prepping in her kitchen and moving boxes at Best Cellars, the more I knew that I wanted to work in wine. But the clock seemed to tick and tick and tick with no return phone call from Andrea offering me my dream job, and by the time I got back from Christmas break, I knew I needed some form of income if I wanted to stay in the city. While my dad had said he would pay my rent while I was in school, school was over now, and I was expected to get a full-time job so I could start paying my own way.

That was when the manager at Best Cellars, Krista, interviewed me for a job in management. We met at a Starbucks across the street from the store, and in the middle of the interview, someone stole my purse off the back of my chair. Krista gave me twenty bucks and a subway coin so I could get home.

Call it a sign, call it what you will, but I declined the position and said I would keep working part-time until Windows on the World called me.

But Windows didn't call.

Before long, the gracious people at Best Cellars recommended me to *Wine & Spirits Magazine* for an entry-level, low-paid position. I have to admit, I was thrilled at the opportunity to work for a wine publication. Now, at last, I could put my journalism degree to some use. Never mind that I would just be organizing wine for the critics to review—I would still get a paycheck from *Wine & Spirits Magazine*.

When I went into the interview, I was downright giddy. I can only imagine what I sounded like, stuttering and giggling, probably using the word "like" like a thousand times.

I probably gave one of the single worst interviews ever given. Suffice to say, I wasn't offered the position.

The upside: Best Cellars didn't fire me for embarrassing them in the process.

Determined to wait for Windows, I answered a *New York Times* ad for a temporary position in the filing department for a small financial organization.

I also enrolled in the Wine & Spirits Education Trust (WSET) eight-week Level One course being offered once a week in the evening at Chelsea Market. It was in this class where I met a woman named Susan LaRossa, a native New Yorker and a practicing lawyer. Susan approached me at some point in the class where she shared her desire and hesitation around leaving her career in law for a career in wine. It felt good to meet someone who also shared a love of wine but was struggling around how to make a go of it. I admired her motivation to take this intense class after a long day of working a nine-to-five job as an attorney.

While I worked and finally got paid something substantial as a temp in finance and took my weekly wine class, I continued to comb the want ads for a job that would suit me perfectly.

Then one Wednesday, I found it, in the "Dining Out" section of the *New York Times*. "Personal assistant to three-star chef: well-versed, organized, culinary background, preferably fluent in French."

It wasn't wine, but it was a million times more for me than the temp job.

If Windows wasn't going to call me (and by this time, it seemed like they probably weren't), I was going to become the executive assistant to a three-star chef. I called the number, faxed my résumé, and received a call for a preliminary interview.

The day I arrived, there were about ten other people waiting in the basement of the restaurant—which turned out to be Union Pacific. The chef was the up-and-coming Rocco DiSpirito, a handsome, talented young man who was already the darling of the restaurant world, beloved by the editor of *Gourmet Magazine* and former *New York Times* restaurant critic Ruth Reichl.

After multiple tests and interviews, I was told the job had gone to a young woman who also spoke French and was writing a book. However, the team still wanted me to work for them, so they offered me a job as head reservationist, with a salary of $40K.

I couldn't believe it! While head reservationist wasn't the career I had envisioned, $40K sounded pretty darn good. I took it—but I lasted less than thirty days. Two weeks into the job, I received a phone call. *The* phone call. The coveted phone call from Andrea Immer, asking me to come in for an interview.

It turns out that when your parents say, "The best time to find a job is when you already have one," they're right.

So, Andrea called my apartment one afternoon and left a message saying a new restaurant would be opening on the 107th floor of One World Trade Center, and there was a hostess position available. I scoffed at being a hostess, but I didn't scoff at meeting Andrea in person. My dad told me to get up there and let her meet me because if I could show her what a great hostess I could be, then I could easily convince her that I would be a great wino too.

I called Andrea back, and we scheduled an in-person interview for Friday, February 19, at 5 p.m. That afternoon, I told Union Pacific I had a doctor's appointment and had to leave work an hour early. I got on the N train from 23rd Street Station and traveled south to the concourse of the World Trade Centers. It was a blustery cold day, and my lips were chapped and my face rosy with windburn and nervousness.

I took the sixty-three-second elevator ride to the 107th floor, where I exited into the hustle and bustle that was Windows on the World, a mile and a half above land. Kami, a vivacious young girl from the Philippines, greeted me and escorted me to the Greatest Bar on Earth (GBOE), a beautiful, vibrant restaurant that contained three bars. I would later find out these bars were the Sushi Bar, Samba Bar, and Shabu Shabu. Kami took me to a lounge area, where I waited for Andrea.

Even at 4:30 p.m., the bar was packed with men and women in suits, people dressed to the nines who were early for their Windows reservations in addition to looking like fashion icons.

What I didn't notice but later found to be true is that tennis shoes and jeans were not allowed anywhere on the 107th floor, so if you made the trek down to the World Trade Center in jeans or sneakers and tried to get on the elevator to Windows or the Greatest Bar on Earth, you were turned away.

At 5 p.m. prompt, the Windows beverage department walked into GBOE and found me in the lounge area.

The team consisted of Andrea, of course, as well as Beverage Manager Mark Coleman, Cellar Master Chris Goodhart, and Alison Junker, the sommelier of the soon-to-open Wild Blue, the new restaurant where I was interviewing for the hostess position.

Before I had even introduced myself, Andrea said that things had changed, and that an assistant cellar master position had become available that morning. She knew I was interested in wine, so she wanted to let me know in case I would rather interview for that instead.

HOLY FUCKING SHIT! My dad was right. All I had to do was go to the hostess interview, and lo and behold, an assistant cellar master job had opened up. It was like the wine gods had finally acknowledged my dedication to the juice, and they were paving the path for my future in vino veritas. Was this luck, fate, divine intervention, or a combination of the three? Whatever it was, I didn't question it, I just embraced the invitation.

I had no idea what an assistant cellar master was or did, but I did know it had the word cellar in it, and she had just said wine, and so without any hesitation, I said *yes*.

And so, the interview began.

They asked me a few questions about wine, mainly which ones I liked to drink. Mostly, the interview consisted of them telling me how laborious the job was and how little it paid, but that if I kept at it, it would be the greatest opportunity and steppingstone of any wine job on the planet.

What they didn't know was they didn't have to sell it.

I had known I wanted this job, or one just like it, since I read the article in the *Times* almost six months ago. Had they offered me the position then and there, I most likely would have stayed and worked the dinner cellar shift. But they didn't, and so I thanked them profusely, leaving with the greatest hope of all time: that I would eventually become a part of their prestigious team. By the time I descended onto the concourse, the sky was dark, and nighttime had fallen. The day had begun with me believing I could possibly be hired as a hostess, and it ended with an interview working exclusively in wine. New York City: where dreams come true.

The following day, my boyfriend, his best friend visiting from North Carolina, my four roommates, and I were crowded on the couches of our apartment on the twenty-fifth floor of New Gotham, watching the UNC-UVA basketball game and drinking Bud Light and red wine from Best Cellars.

The phone rang, and while it was probably not the greatest idea to answer since all of us were pretty loosened up, someone did. Whoever it was, they shouted, "Inie, it's a woman named Andrea on the phone for you."

I instantly sobered up and took the call in my crowded, messy bedroom.

"Hi, Inez, it's Andrea Immer from Windows," she said. "We would like to offer you the assistant cellar master position. I know you're currently working, but if you could give them two weeks' notice on Monday and plan to come to orientation on March 8, that would be great. You will be reporting directly to Mark Coleman, our beverage manager, so expect a phone call from him soon."

Everything happened so fast in that brief telephone call that I could barely manage to speak the good news when I went back out to all of my Carolina family in the living room. I was so excited and certain that I was making the best decision of my life, but I really had no idea how this job would change my entire world: my wine world, my spiritual world, and mostly, the world I lived in.

On Monday morning, I gave my two weeks' notice at Union Pacific. The entire team told me I was making a grave mistake going to work in the cellar at Windows.

"They don't pay."

"You'll never move up."

"This is not a great career move."

I couldn't hear them. I was already over the moon, thinking of touching all those beautiful bottles and becoming the next Andrea Immer.

CHAPTER FOUR

Windows on the World from 3/8/1999 to 6/22/2000

T wo weeks crept by, until one early morning in March, I took the A train from Port Authority to Cortland Street, where I was deposited onto the concourse of the World Trade Centers.

The concourse was lined by fun stores, but I passed them all and took the fast visitor elevator manned by a gentleman dressed in the striped vest that all Windows attendants wore to the 107th floor, where another hostess greeted me and guided me to the banquet room for orientation.

There were forms galore: health insurance, security, fire procedures maps, employee expectations. There was so much to read and sign and process. Next, Ron Blanchard, the director of hospitality, gave us the history of Windows on the

World and the famous restaurateur, Joe Baum. We were expected to be able to recite this history to our guests while being the ultimate givers of great service, just like the man who started it all.

"The answer's yes, what's the question?" Ron would say every single time someone raised their hand.

It was the happiest room I'd ever been in, and easily the most diverse.

There were men and women of all colors, languages, and backgrounds in this one orientation, which, believe it or not, was held weekly. I smiled at everyone, and every single one of them smiled back at me.

This was the New York City people spoke of in the movies—the place where everyone's dreams came true. I imagine that for many of us, just being hired was a dream come true. I knew it was for me, at least.

Orientation lasted three days, and by Thursday, I was dying to start the real wine-cellar work, which mostly consisted of moving boxes that weighed a minimum of twenty pounds each.

The day I started training as an assistant cellar master, I found out that one of my coworkers had left a note in the cellar the previous evening saying she wasn't coming back.

I soon found that this was the path of most assistant cellar masters. The beverage department never misrepresented the job in any way, but most new hires thought more of themselves and their trajectory. Since they were mostly graduates of both college and the Culinary Institute of America (CIA), they didn't think they should have to spend more than a couple of weeks moving boxes and carting wine and liquor from one storage room to another. Others legitimately could not hack the physical labor.

I, to this day, find this to be the most wonderful job I ever held.

Unlike most employees of Windows or of the entire World Trade Center, I had "PA & B1" printed on my security clearance ID, which meant I had special authority to go to both Port Authority and Basement 1—the underground spaces of WTC. They were magical for two reasons: 1) They housed the bulk of the wine and 2) there were so few people down there that I could walk the hallway to the big cellar never seeing another soul. Once I entered, I would lock the door behind me and pretend that the wines were all mine, and for the couple of hours I worked down there moving boxes, binning out bottles, and signing out cases to be brought back to the 106 and 107th floors, they felt like they were.

The cellar in Port Authority was approximately 2,500 square feet, and it held the bulk of the wine for Windows. We had stacks ten cases high of Clarendon Hills Astralis from Australia, Château La Mission Haut-Brion from Bordeaux, La Goutte d'Or Meursault from Burgundy, and, of course, my personal favorite: another Burgundian la Pousse d'Or Volnay 1993. There was more wine down there than I most likely will ever see again in my lifetime in one space, and once I found out my job was to inventory it and put it in numerical order with the numbers it represented on the 1,500 label wine list, I knew I had found my calling. You see, each wine had a four-digit number that it correlated with beginning with 8000. Champagnes and sparkling wines had numbers between 8000–8099; California Chardonnay—8100–8199; California Sauvignon Blanc—8200–8249 and so on and so on. Because the list was so large, when a guest opened the wine list and chose a wine, the captain would run his or her finger along the name toward the left where a four-digit number correlated with the wine. The captain put the number in the point of sale and a ticket would be sent to the working cellar letting the cellar master know which wine to pull.

A typical workday would begin with me clocking in on the 106th floor, where a security guard would check my purse, then heading to the office to see the purchase-order sheet for the wines, beers, and liquors that would be arriving that morning.

By the time I started working at Windows, the beverage department had created a short list of featured wines that appeared at the beginning of the wine list for those who had no interest in perusing a fifty-two-page list. The majority of our wines were sold from this short list. If you were a wine lucky enough to be on this list, the wine was ordered in drops of three, five, or ten cases and stored in the liquor room on the 107th floor, just around the corner from 107 WC, the service wine cellar where we doled out wine to the waiters and captains.

If you were a regular wine from the longer wine list wine, only one case was ordered, of which nine bottles would be taken to 106 Cellar and three bottles to 107 WC. However, if the beverage department had determined that this wine was going to be very valuable in a couple of years or more, they might order five, ten, or even fifteen cases of it—and that's where my PA clearance came into play. Those were the wines that went down to Port Authority.

Then there was liquor. And, oh my gosh, was there liquor.

The Greatest Bar on Earth slung more Absolut Vodka than any bar in the free world, and it was ordered in drops of twenty-five, fifty, or even a hundred cases, depending on the deal of the month. And none of it sat.

Every Thursday night, GBOE (as the staff called it) hosted a salsa night and would easily go through fifteen or twenty cases of Absolut Vodka and five or ten cases of Bacardi Silver, not to mention twenty-five cases of Corona.

Today, I think about the glass that accumulated and how much work that must have been for the people responsible for taking out the trash.

Once I got into the groove, I started clocking in at 8 a.m. instead of 9 because I preferred going to PA in the morning instead of the afternoon. The trick was that you had to be back in 107 WC from 11:30 a.m. until 2 p.m. for lunch service in the unusual event that wine was ordered from the full wine list.

To dine at Windows for lunch, you had to be a member of the club. Otherwise, you ate at GBOE. It was rare for wine to be ordered from the cellar during a weekday lunch, so we were encouraged to read the *Sotheby's Wine Encyclopedia* or update vintages on the wine list, which was the equivalent of painting the Golden Gate Bridge: As soon as you reached the end, it was time to start back at the beginning.

Within weeks, I owned the inventory and the management of the cellar, and everyone knew they could rely on me to tell them if a bottle of wine was eighty-sixed or not, and if not, exactly where it was located. Sidenote: 86 is restaurant speak for out of stock.

Professionally, I was thriving, but personally, I was a total wreck.

I had been with the banker boyfriend for three years, and although we were talking about marriage, he still hadn't popped the question, and I could tell he wasn't going to stay in Manhattan forever. I stayed at his apartment most every night, but as the joy of my new environment sucked me in, I started going out with friends in the beverage department on the nights I worked, arriving at his place after 2 a.m. Not that he minded: He was working twenty hours a day, and his stress level was through the roof.

I should have seen early on that we were two extremely different people heading in opposite directions, but I loved— and love—him, and I didn't want to hurt him or disrupt something that wasn't broken, just not working.

It was around this time that a young barback started hanging around the cellar.

Because I am completely clueless, I had no idea this beautiful young boy from Long Island was interested in me. Even when he asked me to meet him one Friday for drinks with his friends.

I didn't go because banker boyfriend ended up getting a random Friday off, so we went to eat dinner. That was part of being a girlfriend to an M&A person: When they got the opportunity to leave work, you changed your entire schedule because those times were so few and far between.

I had told the barback I would meet him, but I didn't think it would be a big deal if I didn't show up. I thought he was just being nice. If you're thinking I'm a complete idiot, you're probably right. I hadn't dated in four years, and I didn't even know what it looked like.

On Monday, when I got to work, the barback asked me where I was on Friday night. I sheepishly told him something had come up, and for the next three weeks, he snubbed me so hard, it hurt.

But work was always first for me, so I continued to kick ass moving boxes, inventorying products, and organizing storage rooms.

One morning, I arrived to find out that the barback had been in an accident behind the bar: A beer bottle had exploded, and the glass had flown into his eye. He had a hefty workers' comp package and would be out for quite a while, recovering.

I found out which hospital he had been admitted to—St. Vincent's—and called the front desk, asking to be transferred to his room. I'm not sure why, but I wanted to do the right thing and let him know I cared that he had been hurt. His mother answered and handed him the phone.

To this day, I am a super awkward person. In fact, I'm awkward in more ways than one. It's who I am, and I can't deny it. I'm sure our five-minute phone conversation highlighted my awkwardness, but it felt good to check in. I was happy about that.

Spring became summer, and I continued to work with passion and vigor, inventorying bottles of wine and reading *Sotheby's*. The only thing that was changing was the connection I felt to my banker boyfriend.

When I worked evenings, doling out bottles and tasting the minute sips the sommeliers or captains would bring back to the cellar, I'd restock once service ended and then tag along with the beverage department team to eat late-night snacks and share bottles of wine. Because they all knew what I made, they always treated me to dinner, and I was like a pig in poo enjoying the "wine speak," which I was slowly beginning to understand.

We'd go to Odeon, a twenty-four-hour restaurant next to Windows or Balthazar in the Village or Florent in the Meatpacking District or my personal favorite, Clementine, on One Fifth Avenue. The 1 a.m. dinner always included fries, raw oysters, and cheese, plus unusual bottles that only sommeliers would order. It was a glorious thing, and this young girl from eastern North Carolina had never been happier or more intrigued.

I would roll into the banker boy's apartment on 6th Avenue a little before 3 a.m., get in bed, and fall fast asleep. I wouldn't even roll over when he left at 5 a.m. for Rockefeller Center.

We went out together maybe one evening during this time, but the conversation was tense, and if I wasn't interested in his day-to-day activities, he was even less interested in mine.

One morning in June, I woke up in his apartment, and he was still there getting dressed to leave. It wasn't planned or premeditated; I just got an overwhelming sense of urgency to break off our relationship. It was very painful, and my heart broke a little, but the relief of escaping something that was never going to work lessened the hurt.

Now, with no obligations whatsoever, I dove even deeper into my role as assistant cellar master at Windows on the World, the highest-grossing restaurant in the country.

If you mentioned a wine, I could give you the four-digit bin number in a matter of seconds.

If you mentioned a bin number, I could give you the location as well as the amount of bottles we currently had in stock.

If you mentioned inventory, I could tell you the last date the wine was ordered as well as the day it was received or was reported out of stock.

All I wanted to do was come to work and stay at work for the entire day and night.

I'm fairly certain most people at Windows thought I was crazy. Not only was I working all the time, but I was also over-the-moon happy to be working. Most people would hate moving boxes on a regular basis, but not me. It was a challenge that I happily accepted—to be the ultimate keeper of all the wines. Knowing where the wines were located, mastering the pronunciations of these Italian, French, German, Austrian, and Spanish names, managers and captains wanting me to work when they were working—I felt so needed and wanted and appreciated, and for the first time in my life, I was doing something no one in my family had ever done or had ever dreamed of doing. This wine gig was my very own—I hadn't been born into it, nor had I been trained to know it—I figured it out all by myself.

I knew everyone's name, and I spoke to everyone I came into contact with, from the seamstress to the freight-elevator operator to the owner to the security guard to the pastry chef to the shipping and receiving director. Some of them were tired and overworked people who either ignored me or glared at me when I spoke to them. Some of them were curious people trying to figure out my angle. But most of them were simply people who appreciated being recognized and reminded that they were humans who deserved human interaction.

One of my favorite discoveries at the World Trade Center was a Krispy Kreme Doughnuts located at the base, facing Fulton Street.

On Tuesday mornings, our biggest receiving day, I would arrive at work around 7 a.m. when the "Hot Doughnuts" sign was shining and buy a couple dozen hot doughnuts to take to the guys in shipping and receiving. They, in turn, would load up my cart while I passed out the doughnuts.

Everyone in NYC was so used to the local mainstay, Dunkin' Donuts, that most of them had never experienced the glory of Krispy Kreme, a company founded in North Carolina. It was a win-win-win. I didn't break my back lifting a hundred cases of wine, liquor, and beer onto a cart first thing in the morning, and the gentlemen in S&R enjoyed the best hot doughnuts of their lives.

By July of 1999, I had mastered the job of assistant cellar master, in large part because I hadn't quit after a couple of weeks. I had been working for approximately three and a half months, and I knew everyone who worked there from accounting to banquets to the porters.

The sommeliers preferred me to work at night because their bottles would be ready and waiting before they even left the dining room, and the beverage manager wanted me to work during the day because I would have all the wine in the right places with the correct bin numbers and the accurate inventory count before they even sniffed 5 p.m.

The beauty was that I loved my job so much, I wanted to work every single shift. I worked doubles; I worked swing shifts; I worked Saturday nights; I worked Sunday mornings. If you wanted to know where I was, you could be pretty sure it was at the top of One World Trade Center.

And then, what either always happens or never happens, happened.

Barback boy came back to work.

This time, with thick, black, horn-rimmed glasses.

I was surprised at myself when I first saw him in the building: I was a little bit giddy and fluttery. Then I started hearing people whisper about how hot he was, and it was as though hearing it from other people made me actually see it for myself.

Barback was a Long Island native who had gone to RISD. Never having heard that acronym in my life, he had to translate it for me as Rhode Island School of Design. At that time, I'm fairly certain he was the coolest person I had ever met in my life. Confident, easy on the eyes, and extremely open to different views with a crazy wealth of knowledge about art, music, and movies. I felt an overwhelming sense of awe and wonderment when he was in the same room as me. Never in my life had I met a guy my age like him. And the most perplexing part of it all was that he seemed to like me. As worldly as he was, I matched it equally with my naivete.

What on earth was I feeling? What had happened to me? When did these feelings develop? I honestly didn't even know I had them in me.

Barback was truly beautiful, in a way I had never experienced before. He wasn't afraid to come up to me while I was in a crowd of people and start talking about his plans for the next day as well as ask me about mine. He listened to my stories about eastern North Carolina and my family, whom I missed terribly but not terribly enough to move back home. He asked me questions about my newfound love of wine and listened with interest, instilling in me a kind of confidence in myself that I never knew existed. I didn't even recognize myself when I was in these rooms acting like my true self, not someone I thought he might like.

We fell hook, line, and sinker for one another almost exactly a week after he came back to work at Windows.

First, we went out with a few other people from the Greatest Bar one Sunday night in August. We went to Tall Ships, the hotel bar in the Marriott next to One World Trade Center. After everyone else went home, Barback and I stayed on the lobby couches until five in the morning. That was when he invited me to Long Island that Tuesday to go to the beach and have dinner at his grandfather's house.

I already had Tuesday off at Windows, but at this point, I also had a second job, waiting tables at La Madeleine. I spent all of Monday calling around, trying to find someone to cover my shift. When the day ended and I still hadn't found anyone, I did something the old Inez would never have done: I decided to pull a no-show.

I hadn't gone to a beach all summer. In fact, I hadn't visited a beach since leaving North Carolina more than a year earlier, and I spent that Monday night shaving, trimming, and manicuring every hair on my body so that I would look as close to perfect as possible for our train ride and beach trip to Long Beach, Long Island.

At 8 a.m. on Tuesday morning, I met Barback at one of the bagel shops in Penn Station—one of those delis that sells black and white cookies and hot coffee out of the famous Greek cups.

He showed up! That was a good sign.

He led me to the ticket booth and showed me which ticket to buy, then led me to the train. I was in awe. I had never been to Long Island on a train with someone from New York. The entire experience was surreal.

He asked me about myself and how I came to be and what I wanted to emerge. I had never met a man like this one in my life: a man so generous with his asking.

I told him about going to Carolina after high school, just like my mom and my dad did; joining a sorority, just like my mom and my aunt had done as well as my older sister and cousins; and making the move up north where my entire family bet I wouldn't last over a year.

He told me about being Homecoming King at his high school in Rockville Centre; having his heart broken by his first true love; making his first short film at RISD; and, as soon as he could figure it out, his move to Los Angeles to live with his best childhood friend, Eddie.

We arrived at Long Beach, where his sister had left him a car. Soon, we took our towels and the chairs he had brought and found a spot in the sun on a relatively empty beach where we ate deli sandwiches he had bought at the train station.

It was the kind of day movies are made of, and besides the shockingly cold ocean water (I had no idea water could be that cold in January, much less in August), I never stopped smiling. We spent the entire day at the beach learning about each other's families and telling each other funny stories about our childhoods.

He asked me if I could stay for dinner, and when I said yes, we drove to a seafood market where he bought bay scallops, a couple of potatoes, and some squash. Next, we headed to his grandfather's house in Rockville Centre, where he and I cooked dinner for the two of us and his precious Pop.

Things UNC sorority girls are not used to: THIS. Fraternity guys at Chapel Hill didn't have the reputation for being romantic, unless romantic meant taking you into the bathroom at Molly's and sharing a line of coke. In my case, my fraternity banker boyfriend held a similar philosophy to Richard Gere in *Pretty Woman*—he abhorred drugs and never went near them.

If I hadn't felt swoony before, I definitely felt it now, and had I not been scared to fucking death, I would have sexually attacked Barback on the train ride back to Manhattan that evening.

Instead, because I am who I am, I just sat beside him, answering his questions and making sure I asked him at least two to every one question he asked me. I had gathered enough information at this point to know he loved movies, so I asked him his favorite directors, male leads, female leads, what was his favorite movie of the summer. If there was anything my stepmother Mary Ann had taught me, it was that men like to talk about themselves, so if you like someone, just get them to talk about themselves. Of course, she never mentioned that that philosophy worked both ways. He asked me about my roommates, where I had traveled, and where I liked to go out in the city.

At one point during our ride, I remember saying that kissing in bars was tacky. He tilted back his head and laughed so hard I thought he was reacting to something he had seen on the train. When I asked him what was so funny, he just smiled and said, "You have too many hang-ups, Inez." I was crushed.

When we arrived at Penn Station, I took the A Train up to 42nd, where I would get off and walk to my apartment on 43rd, and he took the A Train down to 14th, where he would transfer to the L Train to Brooklyn. There was no magical goodbye, just a hug and an "I had a good time today, see you later."

I almost cried on my walk home. He didn't like me anymore. Once he had gotten to know me, I just wasn't that great. All I could remember from the entire day was him telling me I had too many hang-ups.

Oh well, I told myself. *At least I have work.*

And as a major plus, I wouldn't have to see him the next day and acknowledge that we weren't made for each other since he didn't work on Wednesdays. But I only got a day of respite: He'd be back for the morning shift on Thursday. Before I can tell that story, you need a little background on my daily life. A day in the life of an assistant cellar master at Windows on the World was full, beginning with checking out a lovely and extremely flattering white polyester lab jacket from uniforms immediately upon clocking in.

The jacket had pockets for your keys (although I wore mine around my neck) and kept your clothes from getting dirty from the dust and grime on the boxes that had been God knows where before they arrived in shipping and receiving.

Once I checked out my jacket, I would travel one room down to maintenance, where I would check out keys to the beverage department and 106 WC on the 106th floor and 107LR and 107WC on the 107th floor. If I had to make a trip down to the big cellar in Port Authority or the main liquor room on B1, I would check those keys out too.

Once I had my jacket and my keys, I would go to the beverage office and grab the clipboard that showed the orders coming in that day, along with any special notes about where to place the wines, liquor, or beer we received. And I would always take a Sharpie and a ballpoint pen for labeling boxes and making notes for myself.

For instance, wine or beer might be coming in for a special banquet, in which case it would stay in shipping and receiving where I would clearly label it with a sheet of white paper saying, for instance, "Hold for Gershwin Banquet 8/8/99—DO NOT TOUCH FOR ANY OTHER REASON." A normal ACM would stop there, but not me. I would then find out who was managing the banquet and make sure to find them that day and lead them to shipping and receiving to show them where the wine was and how much had come in, so there were no questions about it if I wasn't onsite the day of the event. The banquet managers loved me for this, and after a couple of months of me doing it, they expected it from the other ACMs as well.

For the most part, however, the liquor, beer, and wines by the glass went to 107LR (liquor room), and the other wines (if there was a case or less) were divided up: three bottles to 107WC, nine bottles to 106WC. Now, sometimes the buyers had ordered wines that weren't ready to drink, and those I took to Port Authority.

In short: There were multiple places a wine might go, and I was a master of all those locations.

My shift started at 9 a.m., but I was always there at 8:00 a.m. at the latest. Then I had until 10 a.m. to be up in the liquor room with five carts and multiple bins to dole out liquor for the five bars. The Greatest Bar on Earth had three bars in the restaurant and one service bar, and Windows had one service bar.

Each evening after service, each of the five bartenders would fill out a liquor request form that told the morning ACM what they needed to bring their bars up to par from the previous night. This gave me a great indication of how busy we had been, and when a manager (who almost always arrived after 10 a.m.) would swing by the liquor room to say hello before going to the office, I would greet them with, "Looks like we rocked the house last night," or, "I guess the overcast sky hurt us a little yesterday."

And sure enough, they would go to their office, check the reports, and find out I knew exactly what I was talking about—all because I realized that the liquor request form told me whether we had a busy or a slow night.

A great ACM had the five liquor request forms completed by 10:20, but I was always done by 10 a.m. I would spend the additional time in the liquor room binning out liquor or moving boxes so that it was neat and organized. I cannot tell you how many times other ACMs would just unload boxes from their carts and never stack them neatly or put them in any order whatsoever. One kid (who didn't last long at all) stacked so many Corona cases beside the door, twenty cases high, that one morning I couldn't open the door because they had fallen, shattered, and blocked the entrance. When I finally got in after asking some banquet servers to help me push, I found multiple broken bottles and so much spilled beer that cleaning it up fucked up my entire schedule.

Anyway. Soon enough, I would have five carts coming out of 107LR, each one with multiple bins (we called them lexicons) loaded with liquor and wine by the glass, along with cases of beer that perfectly matched said bar's liquor request form. It was seamless, a no-brainer: If you were the barback for Shabu Shabu, you took the cart that said Shabu Shabu on it; if you were the barback for the Windows service bar, you took the one that said Windows service bar. You get the picture.

And on this particular Thursday morning, my barback came early to hang around the liquor room while I waited for the others to pick up their carts before moving on to my next important job of the day.

"I remember you telling me about that bar near your house where all the celebrities go," he said when he entered the liquor room.

"Yeah, it's called West Bank."

"Some buddies and I are thinking about going tonight. Want to meet us?"

I can't say for sure how big my smile got, but I'm pretty sure it was huge.

"I would absolutely love that," I said. "Just tell me when."

And that's how the love summer of '99 began. Pretty soon, it would sweep me away like the greatest storm of my young adult life.

During this time in the summer, I lived in the apartment with two juniors from UNC who were interning in Manhattan: one in finance and the other in fashion. Both were never at home on weeknights, so I had to get ready by myself as well as walk to West Bank by myself. I was a nervous wreck. As soon as I rounded the corner of 43rd and 9th on my way home from work, I ducked into the liquor store and bought a magnum of Concha y Toro Cabernet from Chile. Nothing but the best for this aspiring sommelier making minimum wage.

I rushed home, uncorked the bottle, poured a to-the-brim glass, and said a prayer asking for Barback to like me. I then found my newest BCBG shirt my mom had bought me when she had come to visit earlier that summer and laid it out to put on one minute before leaving the apartment. One of my trademarks is wearing my food and drink, and I was taking no chances for that to happen with this Chilean bottle of red.

We were supposed to meet at 9 p.m., so I headed that way about five minutes before nine. He was there already with a couple of guys from RISD who were nice, funny, respectful, and who also seemed excited to meet me. We all drank liquor drinks (something I rarely did, but when in Rome?), and after about an hour without seeing one celebrity, came to the consensus that we should go to another bar. His friends started walking toward the entrance, so I did too, but as I was following them, I heard Barback say my name. I turned around, and with no warning, he kissed me. And holy shit, what a kiss. Like a combination of Jake kissing Samantha in *Sixteen Candles* and C. Thomas Howell kissing Juliette Lewis in *That Night*—yes, that kind of kiss. I don't know how I was able to walk out of the bar after that, but I did, and the rest of the summer in Manhattan felt as hot inside as it did out.

After that night, Barback and I became inseparable. When we were working, he brought me love notes to the cellar along with leftover petit fours from banquets. After work, we would go out with the bartenders from GBOE and shut the bars down before getting in a cab and heading to his place in Greenpoint. On our days off, we would go see movies—his passion, but he also planned trips to Providence, Rhode Island, so he could show me where he spent his four years of college and to the North Fork of Long Island so that he could indulge me with winery tours and tastings. I was

44

so smitten I could barely remember to call home to talk to my family. My entire world revolved around time spent with him—so much so that when he told me he was moving to Los Angeles to pursue directing, I jumped straight on that ship, despite my parents and my bosses discouraging my leaving a job I loved—the greatest job of my life—for a boy. And not just any boy, but a boy I hadn't even known for three months.

Did people call me crazy? Abso-fucking-lutely. And I didn't care. All I cared about was loving this guy who drew me pictures, made me dinner, photographed me on walks, and touched me in ways I had never been touched. I was twenty-three years old, and this decision felt powerful and revolutionary.

And so, I gave my beloved beverage department a two-month notice in October and went home for Christmas before heading to the West Coast with no apartment, no job, and no idea what I was getting into. On January 3, 2000, I jumped on a plane for LA with three suitcases, ready to be with this lover who had transformed me into a woman and to find wine on the West Coast.

My Nana had given me a gray suit from Nordstrom's for Christmas, and I wore it as I roamed the Third Street Promenade in Santa Monica, passing out a résumé that proudly touted Windows on the World assistant cellar master as my most recent job.

It didn't take long: Within thirty-six hours, I had landed a hostess position at Remi, an Italian restaurant with a second location in NYC and a wine bartender position on Sunday and Monday evenings at Third Street Delicatessen.

I waited on stars like Anthony Hopkins and Sean Connery, but stars weren't really my thing, and I yearned for the 107th floor of One World Trade Center every single morning when I woke up and every single evening when I went to bed.

The magical romance that had transported me to the West Coast both physically and emotionally was less magical now that I didn't know anyone and had to lean on the barback to fill all of my emotional needs. I made friends with other servers, bartenders, and even customers—making friends was never an issue for me—but my heart longed for the sixty-three-second elevator ride to the top of WTC, the white lab coat with pockets, and, mostly, to touch those incredible bottles of wine that called to me like a siren to a sailor at sea.

There was no wine community in Los Angeles, at least not one that I found. What I did find was myself acting needy and possessive, trying to make the West Coast give me the same delight and energy that Manhattan did. Barback didn't miss New York like I did, and while I resented my decision to move and leave the greatest job I had ever loved, he resented my constant chatter around our memories in Manhattan.

It didn't help that our schedules were extremely different. I worked lunches at Remi Monday through Friday, and I bartended at Third Street Promenade on Sunday and Monday nights. Because Barback was now working on sets, his schedule was much more sporadic. He could go weeks without having to work, which I imagine was very stressful when you have to pay rent. Our passionate and carefree East-Coast romance had quite literally changed course with the direction of our cross-country move—more volatile and stress-heavy.

I called the working cellar once a week to talk to the assistant cellar master on duty and hear about the ins and outs of Windows life. When Barback went to Georgia to visit his family for a week in April, it was abundantly clear to me that the only reason I was living out there was because of him. This realization pushed me to set the ball in motion for a move back east as soon as possible. Barback knew it was coming, his friends knew it as did my coworkers—my love for Windows trumped my love of Barback, and I officially lasted five months and twelve days in LA.

It became increasingly clear that while Barback was a love, he was not *the* love. The love that consumed my thoughts and my body was my love of wine.

Less than four months later, the beverage director, Mark Coleman, called me. It was early April, and I was at my apartment, getting ready to go to work.

"Our beverage manager Ken is moving to our other restaurant, Beacon, in Stamford, Connecticut," he told me. "We want you to come back and fill his position."

That was all I needed to hear. Within minutes of that phone call, I let Barback know I was going back to NYC, and then I shared the news with my two jobs and two male roommates, one of whom, in a super LA twist, was Ben Affleck's stunt double.

What happened next was mind-blowing. Within minutes of calling the general manager, Glenn Vogt, to tell him I would happily accept his generous offer of $38K (the previous beverage manager had made $42K, FYI), I found out that Mark, the dear friend and beverage director who had offered me the job, was leaving to work for a startup boutique distributor, Polaner Selections.

What did this mean? I soon found out: I was now the lead beverage person for Windows on the World, a restaurant that sold $7 million in liquor and $5 million in wine annually.

And what did *that* mean, really? It meant that the next year and a half of my life would be chock-full of the most incredibly lavish dinners and lunches, where winemakers, importers, sales representatives, and owners of distributors would be vying for my attention to make sure I was comfortable buying their wines.

In mid-June 2000, Barback flew home to Tarboro with me to attend a wedding for two childhood friends who had been dating since middle school—I was a bridesmaid. It was the first wedding of peers where I was an attendant. The Sunday after the wedding, we drove to RDU and boarded two different planes—mine for JFK and his for LAX. We were committed to a long-distance relationship, and I tried to make myself believe I was equipped for it, but the pure joy I felt about getting home to NYC made me believe differently.

It was 91 degrees on that Sunday evening in June when my plane landed, and the warm night air combined with the smell of the river, automobile fumes, and food let me know I was finally back home after a six-month hiatus of cheating on my lover.

I took a cab to 51st and 8th, to the apartment I was subletting for the summer, and let myself in with a key one of the renters had left for me.

The next morning, I walked to Port Authority wearing a cream-colored silk suit my mom had bought me from Banana Republic, and I took the A Train downtown to Chambers Street, walked through the concourse, and took the elevator up to 107th floor. I was home now, and I vowed never to leave my beloved Windows again.

I was twenty-four years old when I started and absolutely clueless about the power I held as a wine buyer in Manhattan at the peak of the dot com age when young men in their thirties and forties were drinking Louis XIII cognac at the bar for $600 a snifter. The greatest ride of my life was happening now, and I forgot I needed to wear my seatbelt.

CHAPTER FIVE

Windows on the World from Summer 2000 to 9/5/2001

When I came back to Windows that June of 2000, the beverage department looked very different than when I had left. With the exception of Mark Coleman, who was two weeks away from leaving, everyone else was new.

Ironically, Susan LaRossa, the woman I had met a year ago in the Wine & Spirits Course who had been contemplating leaving her career in law to pursue wine, was now working at Windows and was getting ready to take over as Wild Blue's Sommelier.

Alison Junker, the sommelier who had opened Wild Blue, was moving to Bordeaux to work for Châateau Lynch-Bages in Pauillac. Alison was one of the few Windows employees in the wine department who had stuck with the program, starting as an assistant cellar master and eventually becoming a sommelier. She had been there for almost three years and was now flying across the pond to get a taste of working in a winery.

But the biggest new meet for me was the new sommelier: Stephen Ribustello.

When he came into the office that Monday morning as I was going over my day-to-day responsibilities with Mark, he looked me over with what looked like a mixture of curiosity and ennui before barely saying hello.

He hates me, I thought.

Previously the sommelier of the resort L'Auberge in Sedona, Arizona, Stephen had also left a long-distance relationship with the intent of keeping it going because he had been promised a sommelier position at Tavern on the Green. Once he arrived in New York, he found out the job had fallen through and had to start combing the streets. He looked up restaurants that had the Best of Award designation in *Wine Spectator* and found Windows. He secured an appointment with Human Resources, who scheduled an interview with the wine department, and to hear Stephen tell it, he got lucky with knowing all of the correct answers to every single wine question they threw at him, and he was hired as the Windows sommelier on the spot.

I later would learn that luck had nothing to do with it—Stephen Ribustello knew more about wine than anyone our age I had ever met.

There were only two assistant cellar masters when I came back, one of whom was Stephen's roommate who had followed him from Arizona. Andre Daher, a big, burly, and super smiley guy whose family owned a breakfast joint in Sedona called 101 Omelets, and John Roesch, the darling of the beverage department, a native New Yorker who was on the management fast track.

There was an adjustment period, for sure, especially since I found myself doing something I had no familiarity with: managing people.

My background at Windows had been managing products: knowing locations, costs, stock levels. I liked that. I was good at that.

Now, my role was completely different. I was ordering the wines, the beer, the liquors Windows needed, but I didn't get to receive them or handle them when they were delivered. Instead, I was told which orders hadn't come in, which had come in but were the wrong vintage, and which came in that I hadn't ordered.

From there, I would place phone calls to sales reps, asking where the miscommunication had been, or go down to banquet managers' offices to explain that the wine for their special event was the wrong vintage or the wrong appellation or the wrong grape.

Between that, making sure the assistant cellar masters were performing at the highest level and were organized enough to keep the two sommeliers happy, and discussing which allocations to take and which to deny, I had no problems keeping busy. Allocations of wine are cases, or sometimes even bottles that wineries and distributors hold exclusively for certain restaurants for one of two reasons: either the restaurant buys enough of the everyday wine they produce ultimately to make sure they get some of the winery's small yield or because the winery wants this wine to be on a certain list (in this case it could be because of the prestige of the restaurant or the relationship the winery has with the sommelier/owners).

Windows had the luxury of turning down allocations of wine versus requesting them as every single winery IN THE WORLD wanted representation on our list.

If this had been all I had to do, I would have been fine, but all of a sudden, I started receiving countless invitations to lunches and dinners and wine tastings—except they weren't just invitations. I was *expected*.

Even so, I knew my limitations. I spent the majority of the summer declining the invites so that I could get my bearings, but when I received a phone call to say I had been accepted to sit in on the Court of Master Sommeliers introductory course in Napa in August, I went straight to the general manager, Glenn Vogt, to ask him what to do.

The Court of Master Sommeliers is an organization that began in Europe and had expanded to the Americas in the seventies using a three-tier course for the top wine professionals in the United States to ultimately receive the title of Master Sommelier. The first exam, known as the Introductory exam, was a two-and-a-half-day course with a written exam on the afternoon of the third day. Once you passed the introductory course, you were eligible to take the advanced exam, a week-long course where you heard lectures interspersed with group blind tastings for three days and then spent the last two days taking three individual tests: a written exam, a blind tasting exam, and a service exam.

The written exam is a huge jump in knowledge from the introductory—many said it was like going from kindergarten to sophomore year in college.

The blind tasting exam is where each individual goes into a room and sits in front of a flight of six wines—three white and three red—and has twenty-five minutes to identify each of them correctly in front of three Master Sommeliers and one timer. When I say correctly, I mean you had to name the grape, the specific region where the wine was made, and the vintage (i.e., the year it was made). No biggie.

The service exam is actually a mock dining room with five tables where one to two Master Sommeliers sit waiting for you to arrive where they can ask you ingredients for obscure cocktails like a Charlie Brown, or best and worst vintages from the Mosel throughout the 1960s–70s, to decant a bottle of 1982 Chateau Palmer, and to open a bottle of champagne while asking you the Tête de Cuvées for Bollinger, Taittinger, and Pol Roger.

For the advanced exam, you must pass all three tests at the same time or you must retake it.

Sound brutal? The advanced portion is only a stepping-stone to be able to "qualify" to sit for the Master Sommelier exam.

Once you pass the advanced and are *invited* to sit for the Master portion, the written exam turns into an oral exam and the wines for the blind tasting are more difficult and the questions for the service exam are even more intense.

This was the path of Andrea Immer, and I was determined it would be my path also. And so, when I received that phone call saying I was admitted to the Napa introductory course, I could hardly wait to make it official and graciously accept it.

Immediately, the wheels started turning. Windows would compensate me for the class if I paid for my flight. And before the day had ended, Chris Goodhart, the beverage manager who oversaw me for the first part of my assistant cellar master tenure, had made arrangements for all of my accommodations. I would be staying at Trefethen one evening, Cuvaison another, and Jordan Vineyard & Winery on the third. It took approximately two and a half hours to firm up these reservations. Each winery already had a placement on the Windows wine list, and the winery owners were more than happy to have the newest buyer stay on their property and get a taste of the wines and the experience it offered.

When I arrived at these wineries, they had cheese, nuts, fruit, and sandwiches ready, plus ground beef and vegetables in the refrigerator and more wine than I could have drunk if I had been there for weeks.

I felt like the queen of England, and I'm sure it would have looked that way to others too, if only anyone else got to see it. But I had no cell phone to call my family and friends, and there was certainly no texting a picture or posting it on Instagram or Facebook. I didn't even own a physical camera so that, weeks later, I could have pictures of my glory developed and show everyone where I had been or how royally I had been treated. There was nothing to do but simply enjoy it.

On day one of the intro course, I sat beside a couple who seemed friendly and kind. Of course, they were, and within hours of the lecture, I had made new friends with Ellen and John Hunt.

Ellen Hunt was the marketing director of a brand-new winery called Rudd, and Rudd's assistant winemaker, Damon Ornowski, was one of the Master Sommeliers teaching our course. Ellen's husband John was just along for the ride, enjoying the course as a little light fun. Back in 2000, someone who looked, acted, and talked like me was not an everyday occurrence in a professional wine class. Not only was I a woman, but I was also extremely young; I had never lost my eastern North Carolina accent, and I wasn't afraid to ask questions of the instructors—often exposing my inexperience. For John and Ellen, I'm guessing they either found this charming or entertaining or both, but for whatever reason, they invited me into their couple huddle and not only sat with me during the lectures but also invited me to a private tour of the new Rudd Winery.

By the end of the week, Ellen had also secured me a special invite for the winery's New York launch. She would be hosting sommeliers at one of three lunches in the city: one at Jean-Georges, one at Daniel, and one at Le Bernardin. She asked me my first choice, and I told her I had never set foot in a single one of them and would be happy wherever she put me.

I was booked at Jean-Georges, and I couldn't have been more excited if I had landed a trip to the moon.

It was when I came back as a successful graduate of the Court of Master Sommeliers introductory certification that my new job turned into more than just managing people.

In Napa, I had met lots of people working as sommeliers all over the country, and when they came to New York for business, they wanted nothing more than to visit Windows, see the view, eat the food, experience the service, and, of course, choose wine from one of the most extensive lists in the country.

In a few short months, I had solid relationships with all of my sales reps from each distributor. Now, my biggest problem was never saying no.

If a distributor had a winemaker in town, they could be 100 percent positive I would happily meet them and taste wine with them. My days got so busy with tasting and meeting people that I started coming in two hours early and staying three hours late just to get everything done.

It was during this time that I enjoyed one of the most special lunches I have ever, to this day, attended for the *Wine Spectator*'s Wine Experience in October 2000. Five months in as beverage manager, and the word was out about me—I wasn't afraid to admit all the things I didn't know AND I loved people as much as I loved wine. The weekend of the wine experience I had so many invitations for lunch, I didn't know which one to take. With the guidance of my GM Glenn, he encouraged me to go with Ed Lauber and Tony DiDio of Lauber Imports.

Not only was Ed the founder and owner, but he was legendary as one of the first importers to import first-growth

Bordeaux into the states. Tony, Ed's dear friend and colleague, was almost as well- known as Ed in New York. He knew everyone in the industry, and everyone in the industry knew him. Glenn explained to me that this was the lunch that mattered the most. Plus, he explained, it was with two women who have excelled in running wineries. "You should meet them, Inez, it's good for you to have women friends in this industry." The two women attending were Peggy Furth and Jean Arnold of Chalk Hill Winery in Chalk Hill, Sonoma. This lunch would prove to be a pivotal moment for me as I would see the healthy and professional friendship of two strong and career-driven women.

I showed up forty-five minutes late for a five-person res-ervation at the four-star Restaurant Daniel and rushed in to find that Ed Lauber, owner of Lauber Imports, had called Windows to make sure I was on my way. Not one of my finer moments. That morning, I had been dealing with a wine shipment that was only partially delivered, and I had lost track of time.

The lunch was magical, and not just because of the menu and the wines and Daniel himself coming to the table. It was also down to the incredibly special visit I had with Peggy and Jean. These women were smart, engaged, kind, passionate, and career-oriented. Peggy and her husband, Fred, bought Chalk Hill Winery, and Jean had been hired as the vice president in 1996. Their relationship was special in that they interacted as owner and a manager with kindness, laughter, respect, and humility. I witnessed for the first time in my ca-reer how two professional women should and could relate as colleagues. Inspired and entranced, I just stared and listened to their stories about working together in California as well as out in the market. Ed and Tony, as you can imagine, were smitten with them as well, and that afternoon will always hold a place in my heart as an experience of a lifetime.

During the lunch, they announced that Jean would be leaving Chalk Hill to be the CEO of Jess Jackson's newest business venture, Jackson Estates. This exciting news had not yet been made public and I felt incredibly important hearing it before anyone else, including *Wine Spectator*, who would later write about it in its November 20th issue. Peggy was so happy for Jean, and you could tell their friendship was sincere and genuine. I had a perma-grin the entire afternoon, feeling inspired by such powerful and kind women in this field I loved so dearly.

From then on, life was a whirlwind of invitations that included lunch at Le Bernardin, dinner at Gramercy and Blue Hill, limo rides to wineries on Long Island, flights to the Niagara Peninsula, boat rides on the Hudson downing Krug Collection, and lavish parties at the home of Bob Guccione, founder of *Penthouse* magazine.

It was over-the-top decadent and hedonistic, and I soaked up every ounce of it, working myself as hard as I could on the 107th floor, then partying like a rock star at all hours of the night.

I'm not sure I ever slept—and yet I still managed to fall head-over-heels in love with another Windows employee, except this time, it was one who shared my love of wine.

It all started in October of 2000 when I landed an invitation for two to the launch of the newest industry business, Restaurant Trade. The gala would be held at the French Culinary Institute (FCI). I asked the sommelier at Windows, Stephen, if he wanted to come with me as it was an industry-only party, and I thought he might enjoy it.

At least, that was one of the reasons. There were also a few others I couldn't help but realize. Since beginning in June, I had grown to have quite a quiet crush on this adorable wine genius who, besides being super charming, was also elusive. All of the captains in the dining room adored him, and it was rumored he had gone out with a couple of the managers late into the night, hooking up with them just for fun.

We got along great as coworkers, although I had to have a few critical conversations about coming in later than scheduled and joking a little too familiarly with fellow workers. The few times I had to address him (which I absolutely dreaded because I hate confrontation), he took it like a champ, never getting ruffled or flustered.

Between his nonchalant attitude, quick wit, and incredible knowledge of wine, I found him completely charming. He also adored physical activity. When he wasn't at work, he was playing tennis, golf, or pickup basketball. Because we were short an assistant cellar master, I would work a couple of night shifts doling out wine in 107WC. It transported me back to the time where my job was so much more my speed, and Stephen would revel in bringing back sips of unicorn wine from the gueridon where he had just served a PPX guest. PPX is the term Windows used to denote the biggest VIP guests.

So, there were a lot of reasons I invited Stephen to the invitation-only event, but the one I chose to focus on was that I thought he might enjoy it.

Stephen agreed to come, but only if I didn't mind him bringing his handheld television so he could watch the final game of the Subway Series, which was happening at the same time as the gala. I said I didn't care, and off we went, taking the subway just a few blocks north to FCI. Stephen was in his suit, and I had worn a black dress with a jacket, leaving the jacket in the office so that I looked more like I was going to a party and less like I was working it. Watching Stephen intently watch the handheld television, talking to the Yankee players as if they could hear him, entertained me as well as motivated me to say or do something that might put his eyes on me. Only when we got on the subway where there was no reception did he finally look me in the eye and ask, "So, what are we doing tonight?"

"We are going to this gala at the French Culinary Institute for the kickoff of Restaurant Trade. There is going to be great food and plenty of fun wine. I'm pretty excited about it," I said with pure enthusiasm.

"Oh, okay," he said, "plenty of douchebags will be there, I guess?"

"Oh, plenty," I replied, not letting him be the only voice with sarcasm.

He smiled and just like that the doors were opening on Grand Street.

As we exited the subway, I thought to myself, this guy could literally give a shit about being with me.

Reception for the handheld came back, and Stephen barely looked up as he followed me into FCI.

We both made our way straight to the closest bar and each ordered a glass of champagne. One of the many areas Stephen exuded confidence was his no-apology attitude of adoring bubbles. We both took our flutes, and I walked toward some other sommeliers from other restaurants to visit while Stephen found a chair to watch the ballgame with no interruptions.

Just like at every other industry party at that time, there was no shortage of cocktails, champagne, and delicious wine. Within less than an hour of us arriving, the Yankees had won the World Series and I had found a cocktail server who never let my flute run dry. Similar to today, Stephen finds great joy or great distress from the Yankees' fate, and on this particular night, he was on team joy. Now that the game was over, Stephen had all the appeal, energy, and sociability of Prince Charming, and we stayed glued to one another, eating hors d'oeuvres from the many stations and giving our critique of each item. The guy was so incredibly witty, I almost couldn't keep up because he was so quick with the one-liners, the puns, the movie quotes. It was a struggle to stop myself from spitting out food and drink while he was talking. At some point, we couldn't hear one another because of the band, and so we just jumped from floor to floor looking for new wines or cocktails to imbibe. The party rocked harder and harder, with more and more restaurant people coming in after work and needing to catch up with the rest of us. I'm not sure how Stephen and I ended up in a limo that night, but we did, and right after telling the driver where the afterparty was, I looked him in the eye tipsy with courage and said, "If you kiss me tonight, I just want you to know it's a one-time thing, okay?"

Before the okay had barely escaped from my lips, Stephen started kissing me with such sweet intensity that my mind, heart, and body all agreed that this felt better than any kiss I'd ever experienced. We didn't stop kissing until we reached the afterparty fifteen minutes later. We made our way into the club where everyone was going and found a dark hallway that was off limits where Stephen pressed me against a wall and continued to kiss me until a bouncer found us and said they were shutting the place down. It was 3:15 a.m.

Stephen came back with me to my brownstone in Park Slope where we fell asleep for a few hours until my alarm sounded. When I awoke, I felt terrified. *Oh my God, what have I done,* I thought. *I have made a huge mistake on so many levels.*

Stephen rolled over and saw me with my eyes open.

"Want me to take the subway with you to work, and I can get on the Path train to go home once we get to Cortland?"

Stephen didn't seem worried or even phased by the night before. Did he not remember? Was it not that big of a deal to him? Did he regret it? My entire being was completely wonky—I felt invigorated by the kissing yet anxious about his feelings around the kissing and completely petrified at this big insecurity in the pit of my stomach.

The other worry taking over was would he tell people at work. Would it be the cool thing to say he hooked up with his boss? If he did, and Human Resources found out about it, my job was at risk. Also, was all of that heat and friction only felt by me? My mental state seemed fragile at best, and once we got going and headed to the subway, I got the courage to say, "I'd really appreciate it if we kept everything that happened last night between us."

"Sure, no problem, wasn't planning on saying anything to anyone," he said.

And before I could even digest his response, he had bought a *Daily News* from the kiosk in the subway and sat down in the station to read the sports highlights from the Yankees-Mets game the night prior.

Well damn, I thought. *I'm getting the big shaft right now from this guy, and I'm a little more sad about it than I expected.*

We spent the rest of the year holding on to our long-distance relationships—me with Barback and he with his Arizona girl—with no faithfulness whatsoever.

I had never had one of these relationships before in my life where there was no pressure or responsibility or expectation. Some nights we went out after work, always with a group, and some nights we went back to his apartment in Jersey City or mine in Brooklyn. We could be with the GBOE bartenders at Raccoon Lodge or the Windows servers at High Pearl or the wine department at Pastis.

Stephen was always so cool and laid back about everything when it came to this weird whatever it was we had. He didn't seem to be jealous about the barback in LA or if I decided not to go out after work or if I decided to hang out with my friends on the weekend. It was a little unsettling at times because it seemed like he didn't care, but then when we were alone together, which was almost always into the wee hours of the night or on a Sunday day, he treated me like there was no one else he'd rather be with, and we shared crossword puzzles, ferry rides across the Hudson, ice-cold cokes from the fountain, and even a bank account.

About a month into our new relationship, Stephen asked me if he could start depositing his paychecks into my bank account. He didn't have one, he told me, and he wasn't really interested in setting one up. Plus, I could help him manage his money since he normally overspent. This seemed perfectly normal to me, so that week when we were paid, I started depositing two paychecks into my Chase checking. How's that for a mutual trust example?

Because of Windows' strict policy on management fraternizing with coworkers, no one could know that we were fooling around after we left the restaurant at night. Honestly, it didn't bother me. I enjoyed the excitement of sneaking around and the freedom of not "having a boyfriend." Stephen was so easy—he always let me do me with no restrictions.

Life was downright decadent. Party after party, night after night. Free champagne. Sometimes in the form of a Krug cruise on the Hudson River, sometimes in the form of a Veuve Clicquot Halloween gala in an art museum. Because I worked regular office hours during the day, I had to be on the subway heading back to work at 7:30 a.m. every morning—but that didn't stop me from going out every single night.

I saved all of my sleep for Saturdays and Sundays when I wouldn't leave the brownstone, where it was now my sister Burton and two Carolina girls in Brooklyn, until 3 p.m. at the latest.

After Christmas, Stephen's "girlfriend" in Arizona, who was also a psychic, told him they were through, and she was seeing a small, southern girl in his future. A couple of months later, I flew to LA to officially end Barback and me. There were rumors in the workplace at this point about Stephen and me, but I continued to shut them down and play dumb.

As we got to know each other more and more, Stephen started cooking for me on one of his two nights a week off. He would go into the market and pick up a protein and then buy items that he thought would complement it. The flavors he could produce incorporated the magical combination of spice, salt, fat, and acid, and I celebrated in eating each dish he created.

Stephen was a natural in the kitchen—no recipes or boxes, just cooking everything to taste. His love for both of his grandmothers made anyone smile, and he would call Grandma Marge in Saddlebrook asking her questions about dishes she used to cook, putting her in the best mood for days after their phone call. It was these nights where we just stayed home, enjoying a bottle of wine one of us had chosen from the neighborhood wine store or one that a distributor had given us as a sample, him cooking dinner while I sat at the counter that I started falling for him where there was no return. The truly, madly, deeply falling kind.

And we both just kept rolling. If he was going out after work, I was going with him. And I really cannot think of a night he didn't go somewhere after leaving Windows. On the July 4 holiday, he invited me to his house in Monroe to meet his mom, stepdad, stepsister, and nephew, and that is the moment I knew we had become more than just hook-up partners. Our conversations had become more than just wine and crosswords, and we both confided in one another about the pain of our moms leaving our dads when we were young children. We also talked about how to make our relationship official without being fired, and the logical answer was for him to start looking for other sommelier positions in the city. I hated this idea yet knew it to be for the best. He didn't actively look for leads, but he seemed to always hear about them, and we would discuss the pros and cons of each one when we were together.

On Labor Day Weekend 2001, Stephen went upstate to golf. I was in the city by myself, and instead of taking the holiday weekend to relax and unwind, I headed to my office on the 106th floor of One World Trade Center to organize the beverage office. It was filled with documents, photographs, floor plans—you name it, dating back to the 1980s. It seemed that each person who had worked in our department before me had just filed these things away and then forgotten about them.

In the bottom right drawer of the wide filing cabinet was a large box containing a three-liter bottle of Mumm Grand Cordon. I pulled it out of its box to save for when I returned from my sister Kate's wedding, which I was going home for in just a few days—the first time I had visited my family since a reunion in May. I was going to be her maid of honor.

When I left late that afternoon—Monday, September 3, 2001—I had completely cleaned out all of the filing cabinets and organized all twenty years' worth of files chronologically.

The next morning, I went to work early to make sure everything was in order while I was away. We had promoted one of our assistant cellar masters, Steve Adams, to beverage manager, and he had barely been working in this new position a week and a half. I wanted to make sure every single work obligation was on paper with clear instructions so that he knew exactly what to order and when (which was the bulk of my job).

The seamstress in our uniforms department had altered my bridesmaid's dress, so I checked in with her to make sure I would be able to take it when I left that afternoon. Stephen and I had plans to eat with a wine distributor that evening at a new restaurant that was soon to open in the West Village, so I needed to be out of Windows promptly at 5 p.m. to meet him at Tall Ships, the hotel bar in the Marriott that was connected to the World Trade Center.

I was so excited to go home to see my sister get married, I was about to jump out of my skin. Before I left, I went to every department to tell them goodbye and to let them know Steve Adams could take care of any issue that might arise while I was gone.

I met Stephen at Tall Ships, and we pounded a couple of cocktails before heading to the restaurant to wine and dine on someone else's tab.

I remember being at this hip new place and watching Charlie Rose get turned away at the door because the opening event was only for a select group of industry people. *Look at me,* I thought. Who would ever have guessed I would have ended up in New York City, buying wine at the largest-grossing restaurant in North America, and moving and shaking with the popular people?

Could I be in heaven?

CHAPTER SIX

The Wedding

My younger sister Burton and I traveled home for the wedding together. She lived with me in Brooklyn, working as a temp at an automated people-mover company, and we took a cab to LaGuardia for our flight to Raleigh-Durham. That afternoon, we were reunited with our other sister Kate (the bride) as well as our brother, Ken, my dad, and my stepmom Mary Ann—all of us together again in Tarboro, at Cotton Valley, the name of the house where we had all lived since I was in the fourth grade.

Cotton Valley is a plantation house located on farmland just outside the Tarboro city limits. It was built in the 1800s, and my dad bought it and restored it after he and Mary Ann got married. Over the years, three of their four children have had their wedding receptions there.

The yard is green and glorious, especially in the spring-time, with confederate jasmine growing alongside the porches and irises decorating the perimeter of the house. There's a scuppernong grapevine next to the house that produces the sweetest grape memories of my childhood when Dad would host a dove hunt every Labor Day weekend, and I would hide under the trellis eating grapes until my stomach was sick. It's only now as I write that I begin to think this could have been the first omen of my career in wine.

Kate, Ken, Burton, and I are to this day a close-knit group of siblings who also happen to be blended. Burton's and my father married Kate and Ken's mother when we were all under the age of ten, and we lived together under one roof until we graduated from high school. We went on vacations together, including a no-parent five-week excursion around Europe that sealed the deal on our closeness.

None of us took it for granted that we were able to be home together as one unit for the last couple of days before the first one said *I do* to her life partner. We stayed close from the minute we all got home until it was time to give our eldest sibling away.

My dad loves to say that we put the "fun" in dysfunctional, and the Thursday night family dinner before the wedding is the perfect illustration. My mom—aka my dad's ex-wife—my dad's ex-sister-in-law, and my dad's ex-mother-in-law hosted the dinner for my stepsister. Honestly, most people don't believe me when I tell them this, but it's absolutely true. When my dad married Mary Ann, my grandmother Nana became another grandmother to my new stepbrother and stepsister.

Everyone adapted, and twenty years later, we were all there to celebrate Kate's wedding. All of us.

Including the old Inie. We didn't know it then, but that weekend was the last time my family got to spend time with her. The Thursday night cocktail party, the Friday bridesmaid luncheon and rehearsal dinner, the Saturday pre-wedding festivities, and, later, the ceremony and reception were the last days my immediate family spent with the person I was before a life-changing tragedy.

That weekend, I was the person they had always known, living the life they had always known me to live: an existence of liveliness and merriment, carefree and care-less. An existence of love for all and everyone, with no boundaries and no bitterness.

Kate and I slept in the same bed Thursday and Friday night, then after the fairytale reception that included parents, stepparents, grandparents, step-grandparents, and the entire town, she and Tommy drove to Raleigh to stay at a motel before their Sunday morning flight.

From the moment Mom and Dad divorced, Burton and I spent most weekends driving toward or away from one of our parents. Now, I was twenty-five, but this weekend was no different. That Sunday morning, Mom picked Burton and me up to go to the mountains with her and her friends so that she could have some time with us before flying back to New York on Wednesday.

And that is why I wasn't in Manhattan on the 107th floor of One World Trade Center the morning of September 11.

CHAPTER SEVEN

September 11, 2001

Turbulence

I wake up to my mother standing over me, crying.

She ushers me out of the bedroom and into the living room, where everyone has their eyes glued to the television.

Only one plane has hit. The North Tower.

I think, *Wow, this is going to be a huge mess to clean up once I get back to work.*

Turmoil

As I sit on the carpet, everyone in the room staring at the TV screen, a second plane hits. The South Tower.

I am confused and nauseous.

I try to comprehend. I try to understand, but I don't know if I am breathing or not.

I make my way to the telephone in the kitchen, and I start calling my office.

Call after call after call, I reach a busy signal.

I try to call Stephen, and the phone rings six times before an answering machine picks up. I alternate calling him with calling my office.

Busy signal, ring, ring, ring, ring, ring, ring, answering machine.

I am in complete panic mode.

I finally dial the home of my former coworker who lives on the Upper West Side.

Susan is crying.

Why is she crying?

Everything will be fine.

I don't want to hear her cry or sound desperate. It's making me angry.

Tick Tock

My mom has brought the phone to me where I'm sitting on the floor so that I can try to call my people and watch the television at the same time.

With no warning, One World Trade Center starts imploding.

I am so confused.

What is happening?

Who is falling inside?

Why the fuck won't anyone answer the phone?

We have to leave. I tell my mom we have to leave and go home.

I need to get home and make sure everyone is okay.

Maybe if I leave this place where I watched it, once I get home, I will find out that it's not real.

I don't want to watch anymore. I want to get in the car where I cannot watch anything but the road ahead and behind us.

My mom's response is a total "whatever you want," but it's too late.

The South Tower starts imploding right before my very eyes.

Tame

I'm not sure who packed, but my sister, my mom, and I are in my mom's car driving east from Blowing Rock, North Carolina, and the Blue Ridge Mountains toward my small town.

The radio is on, speculating about what is happening in our country.

At this point, one plane has apparently flown into the Pentagon and another has crashed somewhere in Pennsylvania.

When we arrive at Nana's house in Tarboro four hours east, my dad and Mary Ann are on her front lawn waiting for me.

"I thought y'all were at the beach," I say.

"We were."

They both hug me, and I guess at some point, they leave.

Now Nana is telling me a woman named Maggie has been calling her house asking for me.

"She needs to talk to you as soon as you can call her," Nana says.

Maggie

I call Maggie.

Her boyfriend Jeff worked with me.

He had gone to work that morning.

She is asking me if he could have been somewhere other than at the top of the building.

"He could have," I murmur. "He absolutely could have."

I start telling her about my friend Heather, who was working that day.

"Sh-she's up there," I stammer.

Before we hang up the phone, Maggie says to me, "I hope your friend Heather is okay."

Who is Heather? I think.

Tired

My mom gives me a sleeping pill.

I've never taken any pills other than Advil and Ecstasy.

CHAPTER EIGHT

The Weeks After 9/11

September 12

I wake up.

I know it's not a dream.

I feel sick; then I make myself go back to sleep.

I have finally gotten in touch with Stephen. He called me from his home phone at 10:43 a.m. on the 11th when he woke up to forty-three messages blinking on his answering machine and a smoky gray view of the New York skyline. Completely disoriented and in a state of shock, he and I kept saying the same thing to one another—do you think anyone up there was able to get down?

I am hysterical and adamant that we see each other.

My mother tells me I am not leaving to go back to New York.

I have no car, so I can't disobey her.

I tell Stephen to get on the train in Newark and head to Baltimore, where I'll pick him up.

I tell my mom we're driving to Baltimore.

She starts to tell me no, but there is a psychotic look on my face that lets her know I will find a way to get Stephen.

Somehow, some way, we get to the right train station in Baltimore and wait only minutes before Stephen deboards. It is like seeing an angel. My mind and heart are now in sync. Even though I had heard Stephen's voice telling me he wasn't at work, my eyes needed to see him to know it was true. The past twenty-four hours had passed with me believing everyone is dead or missing. Being able to see Stephen in the flesh gives me this overwhelming comfort that shocks the crying out of my system for about five hours, the amount of time it takes us to drive back to Tarboro.

My mother drops us off at Cotton Valley, and Stephen and I find a bedroom to go to sleep.

I get into the crook of his body in a fetal position and cry until there are no tears left.

I cry for both of us. He just breathes. He breathes for both of us.

September 13

We drive to Greenville to hear my brother's band play.

One of his friends gets us really, really high, and Ken plays "Scarlet Begonias," my favorite song.

I don't know how we get home.

September 14

We drive to the beach where my dad and Mary Ann are staying.

My aunt and uncle are there too. They have come to be with them so they don't have to be alone.

No one, I realize, wants to be alone right now.

David Emil, the owner of Windows on the World, and Michael Lomonaco, the executive chef, were interviewed by Barbara Walters; they talked about how Chef Lomonaco wasn't there because of something to do with his eyeglasses.

David Emil starts to cry. For the past year and a half, I worked in an office located directly across the hall from David's office. David loved wine, and we had worked closely almost since the moment I started as a beverage manager. Serious, quirky, and extremely wise, I often looked to David for advice in business decision-making as well as my side hobby of writing. In our time together, I had never seen him break like this. And on national television, no less. He looked and acted exactly like I felt: exhausted, distraught, disbelieving, hopeless.

I look around at everyone in the living room watching the television, and I realize they are all also crying.

I don't want them to cry.

I don't want anyone to cry.

I grew up hearing the words, "Everything will be fine. We are fortunate. We have so much. We don't need to be sad."

They are all crying.

I don't think I've ever seen them all cry, even when their parents died.

September 15

It's Stephen's birthday.

We were supposed to be in New Jersey today. At a very fancy restaurant with a huge wine cellar, after his eighteen-hole golf game at Baltusrol, which I had scored for him using my cousin's husband's membership.

Instead, we're in North Carolina at my aunt's beach house, eating catfish (Stephen's least favorite fish) on top of powdered mashed potatoes.

There are a couple of helium balloons tied to his chair.

My old NYC roommate Lindley is there, but I have no idea how she got there.

A friend of mine from college, Joey, is there too, but I don't know how he got there either.

We are surrounded by laughter, love, and safety.

I try to drink as much as I can so that I forget that anything bad has happened. Unlike the times before 9/11 when we went out and sipped wine and beer, there is no joy or fun attached; instead, it just eventually makes me sleepy, and being asleep is the only time where I don't feel completely alone. If it weren't for Stephen being beside me, I'm not sure I could have gotten out of bed the days that followed. My family wants so desperately to help me, but I am beyond help. I am so angry at God and the world. I feel so betrayed. I feel like I have no home.

At some point, we end up at Lindley's house and go to sleep. When I wake up the next morning, I come into the same feelings I had before I went to bed.

September 17

Stephen, my sister Burton, and I rent a car and drive north.

We're going to his mom's house in Monroe, New York.

When we cross the George Washington Bridge, there is an enormous American flag hanging from the center arches.

We arrive at his mom's house after 10 p.m., and Burton and I sleep in the guest room.

"You aren't going to sleep with me?" Stephen asks.

"Not at your mom's," I answer.

The world has gone up in smoke, and I'm still letting southern manners dictate my decisions.

But looking back, I know I would never have let my sister sleep alone in a strange home.

September 18

We take a bus into the city to attend a meeting of all the Windows survivors.

It's held at a restaurant on the Upper West Side called Ouest. There are so many people crowded into the small dining room. It's mid-afternoon, and there is a myriad of different departments represented, including the owner David Emil, Glenn, the general manager, and Chef Lomonaco. The main purpose of the meeting is to try to account for every employee. The Human Resources Director, Elizabeth Ortiz, speaks to all of us about a Windows hotline they are setting up in midtown with a LexisNexis printout of names of all employees. It will have status beside each name: confirmed alive, confirmed dead, or missing. I'm still unsure of everything that transpired in that hour, but in addition to the loneliness, the emptiness, and the anger, I have now added nausea to my list of feelings.

Andrea Immer, the former beverage director and current wine consultant, hands me a grape decal and her Master Sommelier pin to wear as good luck for the advanced exam I have coming up in October.

September 19–October 3

On September 29, Stephen and I drive to Merion, Pennsylvania, to attend Jeffrey Coale's memorial service at the Episcopal Academy. Jeffrey's body still hadn't been found, but his family planned his memorial anyway. I look for his longtime girlfriend, Maggie, who I have only spoken to on the telephone.

Stephen and I sit in the back of the church. He is extremely uncomfortable, and I realize this is the first time he's been in a church since he was a young boy. I cannot stop crying. From the moment we sit in the pew until the moment the family walks out of the church, I cry and cry and cry. Stephen just rubs my back and lets me sob. To this day, one of my biggest regrets is not being able to speak about Jeff at that service. All of the people who memorialized him were family and old friends. No one spoke about his new joy in working in wine at Windows on the World. I would have loved to have shared his new love with the people who loved him most. Maggie stands up toward the end and reads a poem. She is strong, calm, brave, and eloquent—everything I am not. When we leave the church and head to the reception, we are given the *Acoustic* album by Everything but the Girl CD. I finally find Maggie to introduce ourselves. She is tall and beautiful and sophisticated and completely with it. I ask her if I could say hello to her parents while I'm there. She tells me that her parents were killed in a plane crash when she was nine, and she was raised by her aunt and uncle.

When we get into the rental car to drive back to New York, we play the CD, and I swear it is the most beautiful sound I have ever heard. One of the songs is a cover of Bruce Springsteen's original Tougher than the Rest. The lyrics resonated with me then and still do today. We play it on repeat the entire ride back, and I think about Maggie and how strong she is.

In the days that follow, we file for unemployment; we work the Windows hotline in midtown, where we tell people who call whether the names they give us are survivors or victims; we go to breakfast at Dizzy's Diner and take our time having nowhere to go or be.

How did I get here?

I honestly don't know.

Later, I realize what I'm saying is: I honestly don't know *why* I am here.

We have reached out to Maggie to check in, and she invites us to her apartment in the Village.

She drinks a twelve-pack of Heineken, and Stephen and I drink five bottles of wine.

I sit on her couch by myself and sob hysterically.

The two of them talk and talk and talk and talk and never pay me any mind.

It's exactly the way I want it.

We pass out on her couch.

The next morning, we go back to the Midtown space to answer the phones.

Everything is so different now. The sky is grayer, the people are sadder, and even the subway seems to be crying. Everyone looks lost and forlorn and hopeless. Nothing is as it was. Not even the drinks at the bars taste as delicious as they did before September 11.

I'm so grateful for my massive headache, which stops me from feeling the true pain of telling voices on the other end of the phone that their loved one was in the World Trade Center when it fell.

CHAPTER NINE

San Francisco

On October 3, 2011, Stephen and I rent a pickup truck and make our way west to San Francisco, so I can take this prestigious wine exam I had been preparing for since the beginning of the year. The upcoming exam would have been a good distraction had I not already been utterly distracted. Since the morning of September 11, I hadn't been able to complete a thought or a sentence without thinking about one of my missing colleague's families.

There were no good days for me—only bad days and worse ones.

I believe someone got in touch with me about postponing my participation in the exam, but I turned it down, thinking I may stay this out of touch for the rest of my life, so why not just go ahead and take the damn thing?

Our first stop is St. Louis, and while we're there, we call someone who tells us a company called Charmer is starting a fine wine division and is interested in hiring us. It felt good to hear we were attractive candidates for a job, but I can barely remember to put one foot in front of another much less interview for a management position. Later, we stop in Kansas, Texas, Arizona, and New Mexico, and eventually make it to San Jose after 11 p.m. on Sunday evening, the night before the class begins.

Stephen and I wake up super early so that he can drive me to Hotel Monaco in San Francisco, where the exam is being held. I'm fifteen minutes late, a huge no-no when it comes to the Court of Master Sommeliers, and yet, when I walk into the back of the banquet room, one of the lecturing MSes looks up, sees me, and introduces me as a former employee of Windows on the World. The entire class begins to applaud. I sit on the back row in the left-hand part of the room and begin taking notes. The only interaction I have with people is when we get into groups of four or five to practice blind tasting. Since my first meeting with wine in 1998, my strongest gift has been identifying wines blindly (i.e., using my nose and taste buds to accurately name the grape, region, and year). It was fun for me and low stress, which was the opposite of how many people felt, especially those who were trying to prep for the exam. This particular Monday was the first blind tasting I had done since before September 11, and the ease of it came back as natural as could be that morning. The first two wines were an Albariño from Rias Baixas and a Zinfandel from Lodi, and I had named them as such. The only woman in the class, I'm not sure if the other men were impressed or worried. I didn't make any friends that week—only because I was too tired and angry to try. If these people thought I was thinking about passing this bullshit exam I could literally give two shits about, they were sorely mistaken. For all I cared, every single one of them could have it.

We spend the entire week staying with James McGibney, a high school friend of Stephen's who now lives in Sausalito. He and Stephen hadn't seen each other since high school, but Stephen had heard from friends that he was living out west. Stephen called him on our drive across country, and James offered for us to stay the week with him.

"He must be doing well," I said to Stephen as we drove across the bridge.

"Why do you say that?" He asked.

"Sausalito is a super expensive area to live," I explained as we pulled into the driveway of quite a large house.

"Wow, I'm not sure we have the right address," Stephen said.

We put the car in park as James came down the outside staircase.

"Hey guys!" He exclaimed.

Turns out James had gone into the military after high school and invented some type of tracking device in the form of a chip that he patented and then sold to a tech company. He clearly had done well for himself despite Stephen having not heard anything about his good fortune, so we spent that Monday evening eating take-out sushi and hearing about the past eight years of James's fascinating life.

I studied some on Tuesday and Wednesday evenings after class, but I had come down with a terrible head cold, and on top of being greatly depressed, my physical state pretty much sucked too.

On the night of Thursday, October 11, restaurants all over the entire country were giving 10 percent of their proceeds to the families of Windows on the World victims.

Although I am half sick with a cold mixed with exhaustion, and I need to be preparing for the service portion of the exam the following day, Stephen and I decide to eat dinner at the Slanted Door, the most highly recommended restaurant by industry people at the time. The restaurant, located on Valencia Street, offered very few parking options. We follow the lead of all the other cars who parked in the turn lane in the middle of the street because what do we know, maybe this is how they roll in San Francisco. We go inside with no reservations and eventually find two stools at the bar. Stephen is sulking as he watches the Oakland A's beat the Yankees 2–0 at home. I cannot smell anything, and therefore, I cannot taste anything. I look around as all of these diners eat and drink, having no choice but to remember the victims of 9/11—there are table tents on each table with October 11 and Windows of Hope printed on them. I feel an eerie confusion around if I am a survivor or a victim. I don't feel like I am surviving, and yet, I am still alive. I want to go home, but we haven't even gotten our food.

When we leave the restaurant around 11:15, our rental pickup truck has been towed. I start to cry, but I want to scream. I want to scream at God and tell him to go fuck himself. My sobs transform from weepy to hysterical, and Stephen tries to calm me while also trying to find the spot where the truck has been taken. I have given up. Nothing makes sense anymore. I don't care anymore. I don't care about anything except sleeping.

Three hundred dollars and two and a half hours later, we make it back to James's apartment. I sleep for four hours and then head back to the Hotel Monaco to take a test I know I will not pass. Before 9/11, I wanted nothing more than to pass the Advanced Sommelier exam and advance to the Master Sommelier portion. Now, I could care less about any of it. Without Windows, what good was wine anyway?

When it's over, I walk out of the banquet room without speaking to anyone and beeline it to the rental truck parked in front of the hotel. Stephen is in the driver's seat waiting to hear if I'm going to stay and wait for the results. "Let's go," I say. "There's no need to stay. I know I didn't pass, and I just want to get the hell out of here."

We drive north to Napa, where our Charmer rep, Mark Cash, has made arrangements for us to stay at Stag's Leap Winery, a castle-like property on the Silverado Trail in Napa with exquisite grounds surrounded by vineyards. The sun shines the entire drive north, and we blast U2's newest album *All That You Can't Leave Behind*. The album name echoes with exactly what I'm struggling to figure out—how can I leave Windows behind when it wasn't *my* idea to leave? It had left me; I hadn't left it.

We arrive at the winery a little after noon and sit on the veranda, drinking ice-cold Chardonnay and eating cheese and fruit and nuts. Stephen and I sit on the lounge chairs and look out into the vineyards where harvesters pick grapes. No one from the estate bothers us—they let us sit and take in the glory of the vines, the blue sky, and the birds chirping. Stephen and I do not talk—we just hold hands and sip. There is nothing to say right now. As the sun starts to set, I begin to cry. As I take in the beauty of our earth in big gulps, breathing in life, I sob out the death of my innocence—I had aged. Never in my life have I felt such intense anger and sadness. It is all-consuming, and I cannot control it.

Stephen just sits with me and holds my hand. He is so used to the crying that he's unfazed, sipping on his wine and understanding that my tears aren't just for the two of us but for everyone who has ever mourned.

That night we drive to the French Laundry in Yountville to see if we can eat there. Stephen introduces himself to the sommelier, Bobby Stuckey, and tells him they share a mentor, a man named Bobby Fusco in Flagstaff. Stuckey finds us a table, and I fall asleep within thirty minutes of sitting down for dinner. I put my head on the table and sleep for the rest of the meal while Stephen eats alone. He doesn't wake me until after he's paid for our meal, an hour and a half later.

For the next year, if I'm not sleeping, I'm either crying or fighting back tears.

CHAPTER TEN

Where Is the Laughter?

While I was writing, I told myself this was where I needed to "insert a story of laughter."

But when I think about the year following 9/11, I come up empty of stories where I found myself laughing. The year and a half after September 11 brought very little laughter for me, no matter how desperately hard I looked for it.

We flew from San Francisco back to New York City. I am terrified to fly, but Stephen holds my hand the entire time and whispers that everything will be okay.

At the airport, I bought a pair of black socks with the American flag on them, and the word *USA*. It's incredible how patriotic I am feeling.

We decide to leave our apartments in Brooklyn and Jersey City and move in with his parents until we find jobs and our own apartment. The brownstone in Brooklyn reminds me of the life I lived before September 11, and it hurts too much to be there.

In October, while actively looking for jobs, we attend the joint funeral of all the Windows employees.

Eventually, Stephen takes a job at PJ Wine in Inwood, and I take a job as the opening wine director at Blue Fin, the new restaurant opening in the W New York Times Square hotel. The restaurant is a new concept by BR Guest Hospitality, a restaurant group notorious for working its managers at least sixty hours a week. I had zero business taking the job. I was a train wreck inside of a shit show inside of a never-ending nightmare.

Instead of doing the intelligent thing and taking a bus person job at Gramercy Tavern with no pressure, I take this director job opening a brand-new restaurant in Times Square, slated to open on New Year's Eve. It doesn't help that my boss is a master sommelier from Las Vegas who scares the ever-living shit out of me.

I look back on the entire experience with a little amusement, but overall, this was clearly a time when I should have sought an excellent therapist instead of taking a major management job. The positives of the experience were all relational: I was able to hire Paulo Villela, my dear friend and the former Windows dining room captain and assistant sommelier of Windows, as the assistant wine director. I also became dear friends with Laura Maniec and Kerin Auth, two servers who adored wine and ultimately made successful careers in the field. Having Paulo work with me was the only thing that kept me sane. I desperately needed someone from Windows for professional and emotional support, and I adored Paulo, who had mentored me since I started as an assistant cellar master at Windows in 1999.

From November until March, I worked at Blue Fin, never knowing when I would break down. Most of my coworkers were used to seeing me with tearstained, bloodshot eyes.

Stephen, on the other hand, loved his job at PJ's and had made fast friends with Peter Yi, the owner, and Ian Morrison, the Spanish wine buyer who doubled as a math professor at Fordham. Stephen knew I was struggling, and part of the struggle was not feeling like I was in a work family like Windows. He encouraged me to give notice and go work for a few months at Crabtree's Kittle House, the wine-themed inn in Chappaqua run by John and Amy Crabtree and dear friends of Glenn Vogt, the former general manager of Windows on the World.

It was right after Christmas that Stephen brought home a black Italian truffle he had bought from a truffle farmer who had visited PJ's. He had paid $150 for it. On his way home, he had bought a dozen eggs, a box of arborio rice, and a chunk of Grana Padano. He took the arborio rice and put it into a Tupperware container with six of the eggs and the truffle and put the lid on it and placed in the refrigerator. That evening, he broiled white bread with butter and then shaved some truffle on top for our simple dinner.

But the next night, after the truffle had infused the rice for twenty-four hours, he made magic. He took the infused rice and put it into a pot to start the process of cooking risotto with chicken stock he had made the previous week. After what seemed like hours, he scooped the creamy richness into a bowl and shaved part of the truffle all over it. As if this weren't enough decadence, he had decanted a bottle of Barolo and poured it into a glass and placed it next to my bowl. The flavors of that meal restored my emotional strength somewhat, and I devoured the risotto, the truffles, the wine, hoping they might transport me back to the dining room of Windows.

This was the only way Stephen knew how to treat my emotional sickness—through cooking. I cried, and he cooked.

Before work the next day, Stephen soft-scrambled eggs for me and shaved more truffle on top. I wanted this truffle to stay with us forever, but it was almost already gone.

Stephen and I became engaged in January of 2002. We woke up the morning of the Martin Luther King Jr. holiday and took a train down to the diamond district and bought a small diamond engagement ring. This happened because I told him we were getting married. He looked at me with those big eyes of his and said, "Okay."

To celebrate our engagement, we bought tickets to a Knicks game that afternoon followed by a few rounds of bowling. Once dinnertime came, we called Maggie and invited her to Babbo for dinner.

"Wait, you're engaged?" she asked incredulously after we told her, clinking our flutes filled with Bellavista Franciacorta, a sparkling wine from Lombardy, Italy.

"Yes!" we chimed.

"Then, why in the world am I here?" she asked.

"Why not?" we both responded.

And that is how we ended our special day—eating beef cheek ravioli and sipping bubbles with Maggie, the woman we had become friends with because her boyfriend was killed on 9/11.

Jeffrey's body had still not been found.

It is a minor miracle that Stephen wanted to marry me since I cried every single day—great big, uncontrollable sobs that looked as depressing as they sounded. I would wake up in the morning willing myself not to cry, but if I stayed present throughout the day, there was no controlling the flow of tears.

It could be a baby in a stroller, a person in uniform hugging their significant other, a sappy horoscope prediction, a homeless person saying, "God bless you," or just a memory of the face of one of my coworkers who lived on this earth no more.

At some point, my crying lessened, but even then, laughter didn't come.

Instead, I became hardened. The crying had subsided, but I now had a guarded edge and an aloof air that had never been part of my personality before.

My Uncle Jim, who was a Presbyterian minister, counseled Stephen and me for six weeks before our wedding. I remember at one session confiding how angry I was at God. I expected Jim to give me a lecture on why it was wrong to be angry with our Lord and Savior, but instead, he surprised me with these words:

"It's healthy to be angry with God, Inie, because that means you still believe in Him."

I'm pretty sure I cried myself to sleep when I got home that night. I felt so forsaken by God, so disappointed in His leadership, so hurt by His terrible timing, so angry at Him for this plan.

Before September 11, I was a Jesus-loving, party-going, fun-hunting, sex-crazed child.

After 9/11, I turned on God, I boycotted parties, I didn't recognize fun, and the last thing I craved was anything that could make me feel good.

At some point in the summer of 2000, my parents had called me a hedonist. After looking it up in the dictionary, I had questioned what was wrong with seeking out pleasure. Wasn't that what everyone really wanted: pleasure?

But now, my life, or at least my previous life with all its pleasure, was nowhere to be found. Instead of smiling in the morning when I walked to the subway, I found myself biting my lip and fighting off tears. Instead of thinking about what bar I would find myself visiting toward the end of the day, all I could think about was when I would be able to get back into my bed. Instead of making conversation with fellow workers and neighbors, I watched them, wondering how they were still able to smile, still able to laugh, still able to speak coherently.

Had I had any feelings, I would describe that time as painful. But I didn't. I was completely numb, completely devoid of sensation. I was limp, stuck in a deep, dark sleep. The only comfort would have been someone telling me I didn't have to live any longer.

This is how I experienced my life in the months after 9/11.

For more than a year, I walked around in a dark haze that smelled like smoke and looked like airplanes flying into buildings. When I think about this time, all I can feel is the pain of those who had to witness my existence. They must have felt the agony of seeing a stranger who looked very similar to someone they had once known intimately.

I was a walking archetype of a 9/11 survivor: Even though I was alive, I carried with me all of the people who were killed that tragic morning. My face was a constant mirror of that incredible, unimaginable sadness. I have never broken a bone, but my heart had broken open enough to feel like every single one in my body had.

CHAPTER ELEVEN

On the Square

D ad was desperate for me to move home to Tarboro, and after 9/11, his desperation became a mission.

He finally convinced Stephen and me to make a short stop back home during the summer of 2002 to relax and unwind before moving to France for three months to work the harvest in Burgundy. In fact, Stephen helped convince me too. "Why not?" he asked. "We can take some time to figure it out. We're lucky you have a family who can allow us to do that."

The plan was to get a respite before going to France to work the harvest, and then—once I could go a day without crying—move back to New York to get the jobs we were destined to work in the world of wine. In the meantime, my parents were only too happy to have us come home to Tarboro to live with them and help us figure out our next steps. Meaning, among other things, figure out plans for the wedding. Stephen and I were engaged, but at this point, we hadn't even set a wedding date, and my parents' plea for us to come to Tarboro was also in part about arranging the wedding.

We drove a U-Haul down the Jersey Turnpike one morning in May and reached my dad and Mary Ann's house, Cotton Valley, that evening. In the U-Haul was a case of Veuve Clicquot Brut NV with the Windows on the World logo on the back of each bottle. Kevin Zraly, the former wine director from Windows and dear friend, had made a special point to get us a case as a keepsake; it was our parting gift to ourselves on leaving New York. A few nights before, we had gone down to Gramercy Tavern with a bottle in hand for Paul Grieco, the wine director who had been so good to Stephen and me during our time in New York.

When we arrived in Tarboro, Dad, Mary Ann, Mom, my stepfather, Bill, and Nana were all waiting outside to greet us and love on us. If there's one thing I can say about my family, it's that they love family. Besides being healthy and happy, the only thing they want for their children is for them to live at or close to home, which in my case is Tarboro. Stephen's parents divorced when he was young, like mine, but he's an only child, and he still isn't used to the hugging, kissing, and touching that quite literally exudes from my kinfolk.

So, we arrived for a short stay before heading to France, then moving back to the city. Little did we know that something completely different was about to happen.

While spending the summer in Tarboro, a woman by the name of Frances Liverman called my parents' home phone number. I happened to answer the phone, and she asked for me. When I told her it was me speaking, she proceeded to tell me she was trying to sell her luncheonette downtown, and she had heard my fiancé and I would be the perfect buyers since we were in the food industry.

I politely told her that we appreciated her thinking of us, but Stephen and I didn't have two nickels to rub together, and I hung up the phone, praying no one had been around to hear the conversation.

But my prayers weren't answered.

My dad had been listening the entire time, and in that moment, wheels started spinning and players started strategizing. Before Stephen and I moved to Europe for our three-month hiatus, my father had found a doctor in Tarboro who was interested in partnering with him on a restaurant, and they had bought the space affectionately known as On the Square. It was ours to run, Dad said, whenever we returned from France.

Stephen, who was new to the "Holderness way," which he says is synonymous with "shoot first, ask questions later," was visibly shocked to see someone buy a restaurant in a matter of days. He was frank with my father, telling him Tarboro was a culinary wasteland with no chance of supporting a menu dedicated to food that wasn't fried or broiled.

My dad's response? "If you build it, they will come."

Stephen's rebuttal? "I'll give you eighteen months."

CHAPTER TWELVE

France, Fall 2002

While working at Windows, Stephen and I had met a young gentleman named Jeremy Seysses, the son of esteemed winemaker Jacques Seysses, founder and owner of Domaine Dujac in Morey-Saint-Denis.

Jeremy and Stephen shared a birthday and a sense of humor. When Jeremy visited New York in June of 2001 to sell the wines of Domaine de Triennes—a small winery in Provence owned by his father and Aubert de Villaine—we had spent an evening of debauchery at the Hog Pit, eating barbecue and drinking domestic beer, then barhopping until the early hours of the morning. The next evening was a Saturday, and Jeremy showed up at Wild Blue while I was working the floor. He was by himself, and so we found him a table with an unbelievable view of the Statue of Liberty. An ounce of every single bottle of wine we opened was always poured into a glass and nosed by the sommelier on the gueridon so that we would not ever serve a corked or tainted bottle. Often, the small tastes would be taken back to the cellar as a small gift to the assistant cellar master who doled out the special bottles but never got to serve them. On this particular night, Stephen and I brought all the special sips to Jeremy, who reveled in the nose of these wines that had age, aroma, and history.

The bond of friendship sealed itself that weekend, and we stayed in touch with Jeremy over the next few months.

After September 11, he emailed us to ask if we wanted to move to Burgundy the following fall to work the harvest at Domaine Dujac.

I'm not sure if it was time or being in a different country or *je ne sais pas,* but while I was in France, I experienced some healing. It wasn't complete or all-encompassing, but it was something. The email I sent from France on September 25 gives you an idea of what that time was like.

> *From: inezholderness@hotmail.com*
> *Subject: Life in France*
> *Date: Wed, 25 Sep 2002 06:21:30-0400*
>
> *Dear friends,*
>
> *A recap of the Burgundian vendanges: We have been picking for four straight days, and our bodies have never hurt so much. It is a wonderful experience, nonetheless, because the people are amazing and the wines are beautiful.*

Just to let you know where we are: It's a very small village in Burgundy called Morey-Saint-Denis, with a population of 700 people. We are approximately 25 km south of Dijon, Burgundy's capital. For those of you who still have no idea where I am talking about, think an hour southeast of Paris. The name of the winery is Domaine Dujac, and it is a very prestigious winery started in 1968 by a gentleman named Jacques Seysses. Jacques is a wonderful man who married a beautiful woman from San Francisco named Roz, and they have three amazing sons named Jeremy, Alec, and Paul (27, 25, 21, respectively). We are living at their home, where we eat every meal with them and several other young people who are also working the harvest. There are two girls from the Bay Area, two guys from Australia, and two workers from Paris.

We get up every morning around seven and pick grapes until five or six with a one-hour lunch break at one. What we would call a migrant worker, the French term "gypsy." There are many "gypsy" workers from Turkey, Morocco, et al who meet us in the fields each day to pick with us. Without these "gypsies," our days would not end, as they are possibly the fastest pickers on the planet outside of the Mexican pickers in Napa.

The highlight of the trip came yesterday when I got to perform the pigeage for Vosne-Romanée Les Beaux Monts 2002. For those of you who have no idea what I am speaking of, think of the I Love Lucy episode where she was barefoot, stomping grapes. Instead, I was in Stephen's boxer shorts and a Brooklyn T-shirt, up to my armpits in Pinot Noir, breathing in the heavy doses of CO2. My instructions were, "Don't get your head in or you'll die." Many pictures were taken and even a video that you may be emailed soon. It truly was a great thing, and the comment of the day was, "There will always be a little Inez in this wine." Unfortunately, this particular wine is not imported to the US, so only the French will get to drink me. Besides the day I marry Stephen, it was the best day of my life.

The meals are extraordinary and make me jealous of the French lifestyle. Each harvest lunch is a sit-down, four-course meal with wine, shared by all of the workers, "gypsies" included. Cheese is served as the third course, which I am loving tremendously. At night, we have an even better dinner with the Seysses family and our small group. For wine, we are taken down to their cellar—which is bigger than my house (no joke)—to pick out wine for the evening's meal. For example, Vosne-Romanée 1964 from la

Pousse d'Or, Bonnes-Mares 1974 from Dujac himself, or Château la Mission Haut-Brion 1976 (my birth year—très exciting).

It is an unbelievable experience, and I am so glad we came, for many reasons. Whether I speak to you often or not, you are all aware of the events of the past year and the toll they have taken on my emotional, spiritual, and physical well-being. It has been extremely hard for me to process what really happened a year ago and, of course, why it happened. I have cried a lot, and I have been very angry at the world. All of that has slowly changed during this time in France, where grapes are the focus, and the quality of life is not hurt by the evening news and the newspapers. I am working on becoming the old Inie, or Inez to some of you, and while I am not completely there, I think I am headed in the right direction. I want to tell everyone how happy I am to be in this world because this is the first time I have felt this way since last year.

Love to everyone,
Me

CHAPTER THIRTEEN

Wedding and Borgata

When we got back to Tarboro, Stephen and I started attempting to make a go of running a restaurant with a team of six: Frances, Teresa, Neal, Xavyer, and the two of us. Meanwhile, we were also planning our wedding.

We would be married on the front porch of Cotton Valley, then have our reception in the backyard. Tarboro weddings are something of a tradition, and when we had a newspaper, invitations to in-town guests were published there, as opposed to everyone being mailed their invite. Our wedding was no different. Despite our futile attempts to keep it small and intimate, it grew exponentially each and every day. When all was said and done, I believe 300 people were in attendance.

But before that, in early March—about seven weeks before the wedding—I was at the restaurant when I received a mass email from two esteemed sommeliers in New York, David Gordon and Steve Olson, announcing a wine director position for the first casino to open in Atlantic City in thirteen years. The casino would hold eleven restaurants, four of them fine dining, and while the sommeliers would stay on as consultants, the wine director would ultimately be in charge of managing the lists, inventory, and service components.

I ran back into the kitchen to tell Stephen about the email. Without even thinking about it, he told me I should call and inquire.

I knew one of the sommeliers, Steve, personally, so I called him to ask if I would be eligible to interview. Steve screamed, "Heck yes!" into the phone, and told me he would call me back immediately to schedule an interview.

And that was no exaggeration.

Within minutes, the vice president of food and beverage, Victor Tiffany, called to see if I could go to Atlantic City to meet with him about the wine director position. He wanted to see me on Thursday. That day was Tuesday.

I went back into the kitchen at On the Square.

"We need to talk," I said to Stephen.

I have never met a man who wanted me to advance in my career the way Stephen does. That's the beauty of him. Whenever there's a decision that could possibly propel my professional development, he always encourages it—even when it meant us living apart at the very start of our marriage.

Here's what Stephen knew to be true: On the Square could not pay both of us and make it at this point in its life.

Here's what I knew to be true: the same thing. And that I missed New York something fierce. Atlantic City isn't Manhattan in any way, shape, or form, but it's closer than Tarboro, and I would be able to get up there for my fix a lot more easily than I could now.

I called my sister Burton at PNC Bank, where she managed the tellers.

"Any chance you can take off tomorrow and Thursday to drive me to Atlantic City?"

Burton, who has a semi-healthy love of gambling, said yes before city was out of my lips.

And so, the next day, a little after lunchtime, the two of us hopped into her car and drove the eight hours to Atlantic City, arriving around 10 p.m. and checking into the hotel where Victor had arranged for us to stay. The next morning, Burton dropped me off at the Borgata temporary office space to meet the illustrious Mr. Tiffany.

I told her we'd be done at 1 p.m. and she could pick me up then, so we could head back to Tarboro and hopefully get home by midnight.

Victor was the happiest, most animated and excited man I had ever met. Tall, slender, and in his mid-forties, he hugged me as soon as he walked into the lobby where I was waiting.

"Inez!!!" he exclaimed. "YOU are exactly who we have been waiting for."

I immediately knew I would love working with him. We hopped into his car and drove to the Borgata Hotel Casino & Spa, which was still under construction.

He introduced me to all *thirteen* VPs. He introduced me to the chefs and owners of the fine-dining outlets. He wowed me with facts about MGM and Boyd Gaming, the property owners. He sold me the job hook, line, and sinker, all the while telling me I was born for this position.

Before I was due to meet Borgata's CEO, Bob Boughner, we left the property for lunch at White House Sub Shop. I made the mistake of ordering a meatball sub, which churned in my stomach with a great vengeance during the car ride back. Victor chatted incessantly about the incredible doors this job would open for me, while I sweated profusely in the front seat, praying to God that I wouldn't have a diarrhea attack.

When we got to the temporary office space and took the elevator to the fourth floor, he told me to wait while he went to get Mr. Boughner. I asked the receptionist where the restroom was, only to find the door locked for security reasons. I turned around to see a gentleman (who I would later discover was Vice President of Gaming) coming out of the men's room with a key, grabbed it from him, and ran into the restroom, barely getting my suit pants down before my IBS had its say.

At this point, I started crying tears of relief and thanking God for letting me make it. The combination of nerves and meatball sub had almost cost me the interview! But the humiliation wasn't over yet: When I left the men's room, I found Victor and Mr. Boughner waiting for me with looks of some amusement on their faces.

Mr. Boughner led me to his office, and within moments of meeting, insisted that I call him Bob. We connected quickly, chatting like we had known each other for years. Bob was extremely intelligent, passionate about hospitality, enthusiastic about building his management team, and very humble. I adored him instantly.

After the interview, Victor walked me out to the car where Burton was jumping up and down, shouting that she had won $300 on a slot machine. Victor acted like it was the greatest thing he had ever heard, and they screamed and clapped and hugged as if they had known each other forever too.

The whole experience was surreal, and Burton and I laughed the entire drive back to Tarboro thinking about what could have happened had I not made it to the bathroom in time.

The next day, I received an official offer letter via secure email. The salary was 85 percent higher than what I was making at On the Square and 25 percent higher than what I made at Windows. Stephen and I read the letter together, and he rubbed my back, saying I should accept the offer: It was the best thing for me, which meant ultimately, it was the best thing for us.

I printed the letter, signed it, and mailed it back. The agreement was that I would move to Atlantic City and start on May 1, five days after Stephen and I were to be married.

Like Stephen, my father has always encouraged me to pursue my career and trust my instincts. His excitement and enthusiasm were half about my career advancement and half about his love for Atlantic City and casinos in general. Nana was also in the Stephen-Dad boat: She was progressive and wanted me to have the same opportunities as any man would have. She was also extremely realistic and understood that there was no long game for Stephen and me to support ourselves if On the Square was our only income.

Mary Ann and my mom, however, were adamantly against me moving to New Jersey and living apart from my husband. They saw it as asking for trouble, and the next six weeks leading up to the wedding were somewhat tense and strained albeit exciting.

But we got through it, and on April 26, 2003—my dad's fifty-third birthday—Stephen and I were married on the front porch of Cotton Valley by my uncles and Reverends Haywood and Jim Holderness.

Because Stephen identifies as agnostic, the agreement was not to be married in my church, which was completely fine with me, but to let my Presbyterian minister uncles officiate, which was completely fine by Stephen, as he had grown to love my uncles as much as I did.

Our wedding was such a special occasion. While there was no reference to September 11 during the ceremony, all of our special friends and coworkers from New York were in attendance, and the joy in the air was contagious. The sermon used the scripture of Jesus's first miracle—turning water into wine—as the basis, and all of our wine friends from New York loved the imagery around it. There was toasting, singing, dancing . . . all of the good feelings took over that magical night, and Stephen and I smiled and laughed and took in all the positive energy we would need to make it through the next year and a half of living apart.

The following morning, we set off for New Jersey in a Tahoe Dad had lent to us since we still didn't own a car. In the trunk were four suitcases filled with clothes, shoes, pictures, stationery, books, and toiletries—everything I was taking to the Residence Inn where the Borgata had agreed to put me up for six weeks until I could find an apartment.

The minute we got into the car, I started crying. Once I stopped, I stayed dry for a few hours, but then I would start crying again.

What was I doing? Did I know what I was getting myself into? Was I making a huge mistake? I didn't know anyone in Atlantic City except Victor, and here I was, moving to a new place without my husband, days after getting married. Everything Mary Ann and my mom had said about this being a bad idea suddenly seemed very real.

But Stephen wouldn't have any of it. If he was sad, he didn't let me see it, instead telling me all of the reasons it was going to be great and that his goal was to come to see me every other weekend, maybe even every weekend if he could.

We drove the scenic route through Virginia and eventually made it to Cape May, where we stayed three nights on a mini honeymoon before driving to Somers Point, where I would check into the Residence Inn. There was a rental car waiting for me to use until I purchased my own car. Stephen and I were such babies; we owned nothing but some sweat equity in On the Square. He was living in an apartment above Mary Ann's shop that my dad owned, driving my dad's Tahoe, and I was now living in a hotel room, driving a rental car to and from a brand-new job.

Stephen drove back to Tarboro on May 1, leaving hours before I had to be at the Borgata for orientation. It was a good thing as I sobbed uncontrollably for two straight hours after he left. This would be the first time since we met in June 2000 that we hadn't worked or lived together.

But Borgata ended up being a phenomenal fifteen months for me. From the get-go, Victor and Bob decided I was a selling point and shifted a lot of the PR team's focus toward highlighting me. At first, it was local articles in the *Press of Atlantic City*, but when the *Philadelphia Inquirer*'s food critic, Craig LaBan, came to review the casino's fine-dining outlets and wrote that I was a wunderkind, Bob decided to go bigger.

He first had me join him for dinner at the Old Homestead Steakhouse with Marvin Shanken, the editor of *Wine Spectator*. That resulted in a full spread article by John Mariani in the April 30, 2004, issue under the title "Borgata Ups the Ante," featuring a full-page photo of Victor and me at the bar in Ombra. As if that wasn't enough, Bob then chose me to be the wine cover girl as a paid advertisement in *Wine Spectator* and even *Maxim* magazines.

All of this was more fun and exhilarating than I could ever have imagined, but ultimately, it wasn't what God intended for me. Eight months into the job, while presenting at a wine conference in New Zealand, I started to feel super sick.

Stephen had traveled to the conference with me, and we had spent a week visiting wineries, ferrying between the North Island and the South Island and, basically, treating this trip as a honeymoon paid for by the Wine Council of New Zealand. But on the very last day, I was so sick, I couldn't attend the oyster reception for the speakers. Stephen went in my place, and the next day, when we got on the plane to fly back to the States, I told him I couldn't eat or drink anything. He said he felt nauseous, too, so we assumed we had eaten something that had really knocked us off our game.

But when we got back to New Jersey and I went home to my new apartment in Margate and he drove home to Tarboro, my nausea continued. I had no appetite for alcohol or any funky foods.

That Thursday morning, as I was turning off *The Today Show* to head to work, there was a pregnancy test advertisement.

Oh shit, I thought. *I am motherfucking pregnant.*

I drove to the drug store, bought a pregnancy test, drove to the Borgata, and locked myself in an employee bathroom. The second the pee hit the wand, the pink plus showed as brightly as possible.

Oh. My. God.

I ran to find Gale, the sommelier at Old Homestead and a native to the Atlantic City area, and she called her OB to get me an appointment that afternoon.

When I left the doctor's office, I held an ultrasound of a baby in my belly that had been living there for over three months. The due date was somewhere around September 11.

I called Stephen and told him the news. He was so upset that he threatened to cancel his trip to New Jersey that weekend. Part of our agreement when we got engaged was to have no children. Stephen had made it abundantly clear that was not what he wanted, and I made a vague agreement with him that I could sacrifice children if it meant having him as my partner.

It was a scary time for Stephen and me. He knew when we met that I had always dreamed of having babies. I had wanted to be a mom since I had learned how babies were made. However, we made an agreement that kids were not part of our future, and hindsight being 20/20, I believe that Stephen truly felt duped by me.

But God has a funny way of letting us know we are not in control, and nine months into our marriage, here I was, three months pregnant.

Stephen didn't speak to me for about six weeks. If I had known then what I know now, I would have found a marriage therapist right then and there. But even so, he was there that weekend, knowing how awkward it would be if he canceled since he was supposed to be riding with my mom and Bill.

After we told all of our parents, I met with Bob and Victor to let them know I would have to start heading home in the next four to six months. The ride was over. It was settled: I would work until July 4 and then move back to Tarboro to run On the Square with Stephen and become a mom.

CHAPTER FOURTEEN

September 2004: Motherhood Begins

I t was 11:40 p.m. on September 11.

Earlier that afternoon, I had attended the funeral of a young mother of five who had been killed in a car accident. I watched as her babies and her husband carried her ashes down the center aisle to the front of the church. I stood in the very back with my childhood best friend, Emily, and sobbed big tears for the family's loss. Beside us was Mrs. Lee, my gynecologist's wife, and I think she was concerned that my emotional stress might cause me to have the baby right there in the sanctuary.

Now, it was nearly midnight, and I was sitting in our 2003 gray Pontiac Vibe, recollecting the sadness of the previous hours while Stephen was up in the apartment, getting my hospital bag. I was to arrive at the hospital promptly at midnight to begin my induction.

Dr. Lee had confirmed we would give birth to our first baby girl on September 12.

My nerves were dancing with a mixture of delight, fear, ecstasy, and awe, but mostly with delight. I knew I was made to be a girl mama.

When Stephen got into the car, he reeked of marijuana. I looked at him in complete shock.

"I had to," he murmured. "I'm so scared."

He really was. He had been living in fear since the day I had told him we were pregnant.

Checking in at Heritage Hospital that evening was a piece of cake. Within fifteen minutes, I was wheeled up to the third floor and given instructions to put on my maternity gown and make myself comfortable in the sterile hospital bed.

It was midnight on the dot when the nurse came into our room and spread my legs to insert the Pitocin, a small tablet about the size of a Claritin, into my vagina. She also gave me an Ambien, telling me it would help me sleep while the contractions began.

That was when giving birth to Cynthia stopped being easy.

The minute the Pitocin was inside me, I was wracked with incredible pain, and the Ambien didn't help me sleep one wink. I stayed up all night cramping and was in such a foul mood by 9 a.m. that I begged Dr. Lee to give me the epidural. Though I wasn't dilating as quickly as he would have liked, he administered the epidural anyway, and I was able to sleep for the first time in over twenty-four hours.

Meanwhile, there was a circus outside my hospital room. My mom, Bill, Aunt Cynthia, and Nana were waiting along with my dad and Mary Ann; my sister Kate and her husband, Tommy; and my brother, Ken, and his girlfriend, Elizabeth. Stephen's mom and stepfather were also there, and they all took turns putting their ears to my door to see if there was any movement.

In the room with me were Stephen and my sister Burton, since Stephen had already told me he wouldn't be able to help deliver the baby or cut the umbilical cord. Stephen abhors hospitals, needles, all of it, and he had been very clear since finding out about the pregnancy—he was unequipped to deal with anything related to pulling a human out of my body.

For the next eight hours, I slept on and off, but didn't really dilate the way I needed to in order to have the baby vaginally. Around 5 p.m., Dr. Lee came into the room to tell me we would need to schedule a C-section. While not wild about the idea of being cut open (I mean, who is?), I wanted to meet my darling baby girl, and whatever method expedited that would suit me just fine.

They set up the whole operation and got me a new room— but then, miraculously, when Dr. Lee came back to get me, I had dilated to 9 ½ centimeters, and the doctors decided that I would give birth vaginally.

And so, the pushing began. By this point, the epidural had worn off, and I was emotionally and physically exhausted, so within fifteen minutes of starting to push, I weakly told a nurse I was going to throw up and started vomiting into the bedpan she gave me.

It was a scene straight out of a movie, for sure. There was Stephen, pale with nausea and rubbing chipped ice all over my forehead, telling me how sorry he was, while my redheaded, tattooed sister was right beside Dr. Lee with her hands held out, ready to catch the quarterback hike and yelling *PUSH* at the top of her lungs.

At one point, the very calm and very astute Dr. Lee told her she had to be a little less loud so that he could concentrate, but telling Burton to be quiet is like pissing in the wind.

Personally, I have never witnessed childbirth, but apparently, it's quite interesting. According to the email Burton sent the entire staff of PNC Bank the following day, "It is one of the most beautiful yet grossest experiences: shit and blood coming out of every crevice, but ultimately a beautiful baby comes out too."

I'm so fortunate to come from a small town where every single bank employee knew who she was talking about.

At 6:06 p.m., Cynthia Simmons Ribustello came into the world as quietly as angels tiptoeing, and before I could even hold her, Burton cut the umbilical cord and announced to the entire room that our baby girl was born.

The next seconds passed in slow motion living: I could see the room but I couldn't hear any voices. Then all of a sudden, a commotion began whirling around me and everything was spinning. Had I not been so tired and out of it, I would have known something was seriously wrong, but all I could do was close my eyes and think about this baby girl who had been born on September 12. She was a miracle—she had been sent to me by the angels who had left this world three years and one day ago. I could feel myself becoming whole again.

For those unfamiliar with what happens after childbirth, the mother is moved to another room to recover once the baby arrives. When the nurses told Stephen they were moving me, he took this as his opportunity to go into the lobby, where the extended family were waiting, and pop a magnum of champagne he had been chilling. The idea was to bring everyone into the room for a sparkling celebration as soon as I was in my new bed and sitting up.

But that didn't happen.

Instead, when the nurse tried to get me out of bed, I fainted from the blood loss.

When I woke up, the room was pitch black, and I was hooked up to monitors. Stephen was right beside me, trembling with fear. Dr. Lee was in the room with us, talking quietly yet sternly about getting Cynthia a blood transfusion. We needed to sign some papers saying we authorized the transfusion from Virginia Beach or Norfolk or someplace in the great state of Virginia. I nodded to Stephen to make it happen, and then I fell back asleep.

It would be later when I learned Stephen's fear around having children was related to something happening to me during childbirth. He would later tell me that in these moments, all of his worst fears felt so real—Cynthia and I dying together, and leaving him truly alone.

The next morning when I woke up, the transfusion was complete, and I had gotten my blood back too. The nurses brought me my baby girl, and I got to hold Cynthia for the first time ever.

Of course, everyone wanted to hold her, especially Stephen's mom, who had driven down from New York and would be leaving in a couple of days. Stephen is her only son, and this was her first and possibly only grandchild. Not only that, but it was a girl! She was enamored. And I was perfectly happy to share Cynthia with anyone who wanted to hold her.

To me, she represented so many things: joy, unconditional love, hope, but mostly healing. My heart had been so fucked up for three years, but the second she was born, it felt whole again. That's why, as long as I was in the same room as Cynthia, I didn't mind who was holding her. I wanted to share that healing with anyone else who needed it. And I suspected that everyone, whether they admitted it or not, needed a little healing.

And there was another feeling I experienced the minute Cynthia was born—one I had never experienced before: worry. I had never worried before. Especially after 9/11, I was a firm believer that whatever happened was meant to happen, and even if I didn't like it, I had no control over it happening anyway. I didn't believe in control and still don't, so worry just wasn't how I rolled. But now I was responsible for this whole new person. I had to feed her, shelter her, hold her. I even felt like I had to breathe for her. This worry about taking care of her started at her birth and, while it's not as intense as it was then, I still carry it today, for both of my children.

Even at twenty-eight years old, Stephen and I were babies, and we had never taken care of anything even close to a tiny infant. At that point, we still lived in the small apartment in downtown Tarboro, above Mary Ann's gift shop and across the street from On the Square. We still had only one car, the beloved Pontiac Vibe, but this location was uber-convenient for walking almost anywhere we needed to go.

Because of the blood transfusion, I was allowed to stay at Heritage Hospital an extra night, which meant the day we left was Stephen's twenty-ninth birthday. We drove home, took Cynthia to see her crib, which was nestled into a closet-like office next to our bedroom, and I dressed her in one of the many dresses given to me by family friends who were almost as excited about her arrival as I was.

Once we were alone in the apartment, I had no idea what to do. I just held her next to my chest, where I could hear her breathing. It struck me as the strangest thing—to feel so alone at that moment, even with a human attached to me.

We had planned the induction for a Sunday so Stephen could be off work from Monday to Wednesday.

While On the Square was open for lunch five days a week, we only served dinner on Thursday, Friday, and Saturday nights. On Wednesday afternoon, the night crew came in to prep for the weekend, but Stephen stayed home this particular Wednesday for the first time in our restaurant's tenure.

But on Thursday morning, he had to go in, and even though he would only be across the street, I choked up as he walked down the stairs.

The apartment was not big by any stretch, but there was plenty of room—certainly more than in our previous apartment in Inwood. Even so, I was overwhelmed with claustrophobia. I felt like the walls were closing in around me and the only thing that would save me was having another adult in the apartment beside me.

Breastfeeding was not my forte. In fact, I absolutely hated it. And to make matters worse, nine out of ten times, Cynthia would projectile vomit what seemed like gallons of my milk that I fed her. Then there was the curious emptiness I would feel after feeding her. I'm not sure anyone ever tells you about some of the very powerful emotions you might feel once you become a mother. The four I remember distinctly are worry, loneliness, claustrophobia, and emptiness. I had to really work to not let these feelings take over when it was just Cynthia and me in the apartment.

Now, almost seventeen years later, I realize my antidote to those feelings was to never be alone. From the minute Stephen left for work, I put Cynthia in a stroller and walked her five blocks north to Nana's house, where I would have breakfast with my eighty-five-year-old grandmother as she sang and clapped and admired little Cynthia.

Most mornings, my mother would stop in on her way to work at the clinic, so I would enjoy some time with her also. Then, we'd stroll back downtown around 10:30 a.m. to stop in at Rusty's, the gift shop Mary Ann ran under our apartment, where we would almost always find my dad as well. The excitement and joy this baby girl brought to so many brought joy to me too. I was born to share and spread happiness, and if I had known how easily a baby could do that, I might have started having children at a very young age.

My sister Burton lived in the apartment right beside us, and though she worked a nine-to-five job, she was always home at 5:05. She spent most nights in the apartment with us, eating dinner and watching television. This was at the beginning of *Grey's Anatomy*, *Desperate Housewives*, and my all-time favorite, *Veronica Mars*, so we immersed ourselves in TV as an escape from breastfeeding, the witching hour, and discussion of all things baby.

Stephen's gifts come in many, many shapes and forms, and one of them is his love for guests at any and all times. Because of this, he was just as happy as I was to welcome Burton—and, for that matter, anyone else who wanted to come upstairs to a small apartment with a newborn. Of course, there was always good wine available too.

About a month into our parenting journey, something happened that has become a classic story in our family.

While I adore being a mother, it's no secret that I also adore working, and I became a tad jealous seeing Stephen leave for work six days a week. On one particular Saturday afternoon in October, he asked me if I would be interested in going in that evening to run the restaurant.

"Would I?!" I exclaimed. "Absolutely, what's the occasion?"

Well, the occasion was that the Yankees were playing, and Stephen loves the New York Yankees like Peter loves the Lord, as we say in the South.

Stephen was extremely nervous about taking care of Cynthia by himself, but getting to stay home and watch the Yankees was worth the fear, and so, after writing everything down and going over it explicitly, I left the apartment and walked across the street to open the restaurant for the kitchen staff and prepare for the evening.

On Saturdays, Stephen and I would go in at 2 p.m. to let the kitchen staff in to start prepping. During this time before the restaurant opened, we called all the people who had left messages asking for reservations and logged them on our reservation system, which at the time was a piece of paper with a grid we printed on it, in a binder with a pencil and eraser attached to it. Then we would organize the wine room (an ongoing process that never seemed to be complete), count the register drawer, and get a deposit ready for Monday morning, along with other administrative whatnots.

It felt incredibly invigorating to be back at work, and by the time the night servers arrived at 4:15, I was in full hospitality mode, ready to wine and dine all of the guests who came in at the highest level of service imaginable.

At On the Square, we had many opportunities to distinguish ourselves and make ourselves unique. No one in our town, or possibly our region, had tasted anything like Stephen's food. And fortunately for him, an experienced chef had moved to Tarboro to help his parents restore an old home, so while the majority of the kitchen crew were high school kids, he had one professional sauté cook in his mid-forties to help anchor the menu. Our front-of-house team was all women born and bred in Tarboro, most of them teachers or in graduate or nursing school.

In the beginning, almost everyone who worked with us ate their steak well done with A.1. or ketchup and ate primarily at restaurants where the servers called you "honey" and "sugar." Stephen and I dedicated our time to our staff, feeding them foods they had never heard of or even dared to try and creating sophisticated steps of service that were like nothing they had ever experienced. And while I could definitely make our servers madder than hell with my constant refrain of, "This is how it's done at On the Square," tonight they were excited to see me and glad I was there to oversee the dining room.

If there's one thing I've learned about managing people, it's this: They don't like you when you're there, and they don't like the machine when you're gone. It's one of the most difficult jobs out there, and to all you managers reading this: I feel your pain.

From 4:15 until the first reservation at 5:30, we polished silver, polished glassware, reset any tables whose linen had been taken off the night before, went over menu changes, and dialed in wine-by-the-glass descriptions. We would also use the pre-shift to go over what we had seen on the floor the previous evening. Among our many requests, we did not tolerate gum chewing, hands in the pockets, a cell phone anywhere on you, kneeling at tables, introducing yourself by name, picking up glasses at their rim, carrying silver without a plate . . . the list was a mile long.

Offering this kind of service might have been more stressful than working any other restaurant east of Raleigh, but it paid off. It became very evident early on that people enjoyed the service they found at On the Square as much as they enjoyed Stephen's delicious food, and they tipped accordingly.

And because of the money these young women were making, they trusted me and the directions I gave them.

This particular Saturday evening started no differently than any other, with the 5:30 reservations poking their heads in the door at 5:15 to see if it was okay to be seated a little bit early. Sometimes it was, and sometimes it wasn't—it just depended on where we were in the process of setting up the dining room.

In the early stages, we didn't have liquor, so we didn't have a bartender. My primary jobs were to seat guests, pour wine and beer behind the bar for the servers, run the register, and answer the phone. If it got busy and guests had to sit at the bar because there were no tables, I also served the bar guests. If it got busy and the joint was hoppin', as they say—and it always did and always was—the night would end almost as quickly as it began.

So, the doors opened, I started seating guests, the young ladies started taking drink orders, and I headed back behind the bar to pour the five wines by the glass and the two beers on tap.

At around 6 p.m., the phone rang, and almost before I could say, "Good evening, On the Square," I was interrupted by a panicked Stephen.

"How does this work?" he asked.

"How does what work?" I asked.

Stephen was stammering. "Sh-she's hungry. I need to feed her."

"That's a great idea, and I think you should. There are the Medela bottles in the fridge where I showed you. Warm one up and give it to her." There was no shortage of irritation in my voice, and Stephen could hear it.

"I'm aware of that, Inez, but these bottles all have caps on them. Is she supposed to sip from them? I've never seen you do that."

At this point, I was dying. She was three weeks old. Of course, she couldn't sip! How in the world could he not know to put a nipple on a bottle for a baby?

"No, honey, of course, she can't sip out of that bottle," I said, in complete earnest. "You have to pour the milk all over your breasts and let her lick it off."

"Fuck you, Inez. I'm serious, and the Yankees are coming back on right now."

"Put a nipple on the bottle, moron," I said. "How can you not know that?" And I hung up.

The night ended as quickly as it began, and in true OTS fashion, once the customers had gone and the dining room was immaculate, the front-of-house servers and I sat down at the bar and highlighted the best and the worst of the evening. Of course, I had to share the story of Stephen calling to ask how to feed Cynthia from the capped Medela bottles, and we all cried from laughing so hard.

These moments of sharing brought out the camaraderie in our team. By bonding over serving our customers—and, of course, sharing personal stories too—we strengthened our unified vision of what hospitality meant at our restaurant.

Walking home that night, crossing St. James Street to walk up the back alley stairs to our apartment, I knew that next weekend I would be working full-time again. I just couldn't be away for too long. Service was a part of my early adult DNA—it was in my blood.

CHAPTER FIFTEEN

Master Sommelier Path

You might remember that in summer 2000, I traveled to Napa to take the introductory course in the Master Sommelier program. Kindergarten level.

The advanced level was the equivalent of sophomore year of college, with no adequate instruction between the two. The test has three parts—a written exam, a tasting exam, and a service exam—and to successfully get the advanced pin, you have to pass all three parts at one time.

When Stephen and I drove across the country in October of 2001 for me to take the advanced test for the first time, I only passed the tasting portion. I waited two years to try again, and in 2003, I passed the tasting and the service parts. The following year, I gave birth to Cynthia, so it was another year and a half before I went back to try again at achieving this goal I had hypnotized myself into believing I needed to pass in order to be successful in the wine world.

And so, in the summer of 2005, I flew up to New York with Cynthia in tow, handed her off to Stephen's mom, Yia Yia, at JFK Airport, and took a cab to the city, where I stayed with my cousin Zelle in her apartment on the Upper West Side.

On Monday morning, I would make my way across Central Park to the banquet room of a hotel on the Upper East Side, where we would be instructed by six to eight master sommeliers on supplemental knowledge of the worldly wine regions mixed with the blind tasting of two wines. I knew the drill backward and forward, and on our lunch breaks, groups of us would take our note cards and call out study questions to one another, all of us manic about this crazy difficult exam.

Tuesday morning was no different, but Wednesday was only a half-day of education, as the written portion of the exam was given Wednesday afternoon. Thursday was our tasting day: We were assigned a twenty-five-minute slot to come into a room and identify six wines—three whites and three reds—including the grape or grapes they were made from, the region where they were grown, and the vintage or year they were harvested.

Sound intense? Well, it absolutely fucking is.

Friday was the service portion. This consisted of five candidates going into a mock dining room and performing wine service: decanting an older bottle of red, opening and pouring champagne flawlessly, editing a wine list, answering questions about the ingredients and quantities in obscure cocktails, and, of course, my personal favorite, a math question about wine costs. All of us were in suits and, in my case, always uncomfortable shoes.

My friend Laura Maniec, who was taking the exam with me this time, had been scarred by her earlier attempt when she ran out of the service exam sobbing because of nerves, exhaustion, and the downright fear of failing. For my part, I don't test well on written exams and never have.

I met Yia Yia, Cynthia, Zelle, Maggie, Laura, and a bunch of other candidates at Blue Fin, the restaurant where Laura and I had met working together after 9/11, but flew home before hearing the results in person. When Cynthia and I arrived at Raleigh-Durham Airport around 4:30, I had a voicemail from Greg Harrington, my old boss at Blue Fin, telling me that once again, I had failed the written exam.

I was disappointed and a little defeated, but I knew the hardest part would be breaking the news to all the people in Tarboro who knew where I was going and what I was doing and who were anxiously awaiting the outcome. My father wanted it so badly for me. He was convinced that if Stephen and I could become the first husband and wife master sommelier couple, we would put Tarboro on the map and make the town of Tarboro the major destination he dreamed of.

Stephen, a chip off the Kevin Zraly block, didn't give a rat's ass about formal education, especially not wine education, and he made it clear to my dad that he had no interest in pursuing the master sommelier route.

But my dad rarely took no for an answer, and one evening when they were playing poker with a bunch of men, my dad picked the introductory course as the bet. If my dad won, Stephen had to agree to go take the introductory exam.

I wasn't there, so I have no idea what actually happened, but apparently, it was a fierce, drawn-out, and emotional poker game, which Stephen ultimately won. The story Stephen tells is that my dad looked so heartbroken at the end that Stephen said, "Fuck it, I'll go take the exam, Rusty."

Very much unlike me, Stephen is an excellent test taker and an amazing all-around holder of knowledge. He reads all the time, mostly news and sports, and once he reads something, he doesn't forget it. Sometime after I failed my advanced test for the third time, he flew up to New York to take the introductory level—and scored the highest grade on the written exam.

The outcome: The following spring, he received a letter from the Court of Master Sommeliers saying he had won the Michael Bonaccorsi Scholarship and would be flown to England, all expenses paid, to take the advanced exam overseas.

Meanwhile, I had applied to go to Cincinnati, Ohio, to take the advanced exam again. Between mothering an eighteen-month-old, working full-time at On the Square, and studying, I barely knew my own name. But I was committed to passing this exam, and after working days and nights at the restaurant, I would get home and log onto my Hotmail account to read and answer sample questions from my sommelier community, which reached all over the United States.

For me, memorization was crucial. Rarely could I read a paragraph and discern what the exact answer should be. I needed the sample questions, needed to understand how the test would be phrased so that I didn't mistakenly give the wrong answer to a question I knew but hadn't understood.

From the moment in August when I got back from New York and heard the results until the following July, when I flew to Cincinnati (the first time I had been away from Cynthia for seven days), I studied wine, beer, sake, and cocktails with incredible diligence and devotion. And all of the servers at On the Square knew almost as much as I did, as I would spew knowledge about any and everything to them while they were working to ensure I forgot nothing.

Stephen studied too, but it came more easily for him. He could retain so much more, and he mostly studied by reading, while I made notecards and sample tests and drew maps on poster boards.

Meanwhile, we had bought our first house: a small two-bedroom home in the historic district, on the corner of Main and Battle Avenues. It was two blocks from Nana, and although life was super chaotic, Cynthia and I strolled to visit her every single day. One of the most precious gifts to come from 9/11 is that it pushed me to move home and be with my namesake for the last nine years of her life, letting her share heavenly moments with her great-grandchildren.

For me, having a million irons in the fire at all times was a coping mechanism. I had been doing it since I was five years old as a way to avoid focusing on my parents' divorce. The busier I was, the better my head and my heart were, so working full-time, being a mom, being a daughter, a granddaughter, a wife, and a student came very naturally. Of course, we all know balls get dropped when you're trying to be all things to all people, and little did I know then that my role as wife was the one I was failing in the most.

In fact, Stephen didn't know it either, and as I'll share later, that was a recipe for a ten-year braise of marriage organs—mostly heart, but some others as well. Our love for one another was never an issue, but between the trauma of our childhoods, 9/11, and a very unexpected pregnancy, our marriage toolboxes stayed pretty depleted.

We worked together, we parented together, we studied together, and we tried to heal together, but we weren't doctors of any kind, and we didn't have the right utensils to do the necessary healing, not just from the trauma of 9/11 but from the trauma of watching in real-time as our parents said *I don't* to each other.

But back then, we didn't know the trouble we were in; we were just trying to pass the sommelier exams. Stephen flew to London first and traveled north to a small town where he stayed at a country inn on a golf course for a week, attending the same instruction classes I was used to, except instructed by British Master Sommeliers. He was one of four Americans to receive the Bonaccorsi Scholarship.

He passed the written exam and the tasting portion but failed the service exam. Not at all surprising, since he had left the floor of Windows five years prior and had been cooking in a kitchen ever since. He came back to Tarboro inspired to go back and pass the exam as soon as he had a chance, which would be the following year since the rules only allow the exam to be taken once a year.

I flew out to Cincinnati ten days later, committed to passing the written portion and finally getting the go-ahead to start studying for the master sommelier exam, the penultimate goal.

I was rooming with a woman named Julia, who I had met at sommelier competitions in Florida. She lived in Greensboro, and she and I had become fast friends and study partners. We met at the Cincinnati airport and shared a cab to the hotel where the exam was being held. This would be her second attempt at the advanced level.

As was always the case with these week-long trips, I quickly made a network of people I would study with throughout the week after instruction ended at 5 p.m. And because I believed that going to a man's hotel room was not a great idea, I chose only to work with those who would study in the hotel lobby.

The night before the written exam, a young guy said he had a copy of the actual test from someone who had taken it in the spring if we wanted to go up to his room to see it or make a copy.

Julia and I declined. I had come too far to cheat, and if I would cheat on a wine exam, of all things, what kind of person would I be?

Wednesday, Thursday, and Friday were the usual scheduled exams: written, service, and tasting, in that order.

Julia and I both had morning tastings on Friday, so we drove to the wine store on the way to our 10 a.m. scheduled times, where we each picked up a 187ml bottle of Italian Pinot Grigio. This was a trick of the professional tasters: Drink the highest-acidity wine you can find before your test to calibrate your taste buds' ability to correctly assess acid. Who knows if it really works? I *do* know that it gave me a little liquid courage to help me not poop my pants during those twenty-five minutes of intense judging.

The tasting portion of the exam goes like this: The candidate goes into a banquet room where there are four master sommeliers, three of whom sit at a long table facing the candidate and one of whom sits in the corner, holding a timer. The candidate sits at a small desk set with a circular sheet of six wines: three whites and three reds. Once the candidate picks up the first glass, the time begins, and the candidate has twenty-five minutes to deduce what the six wines are, which as I mentioned means the grape or grapes they're made from, the region they're from, and the year the grapes were harvested.

What I didn't mention earlier is that nailing these six wines isn't the only thing that affects whether you pass or fail. In fact, it's possible to get all of the wines correct and still not pass tasting.

How?

The candidate is also judged on "markers"—for example, if the judges have decided that the "markers" of the Chianti Classico Riserva 2000 are cranberry, leather, sour cherry, tobacco leaf, and anise, the candidate *must* say these exact words when describing the wine. If you were to say bing cherry, redcurrant, sandalwood, pencil box, and brushed sage, then announce that the wine was the Chianti Classico Riserva 2000, you wouldn't pass for that wine.

Today, I know what a bunch of horseshit this is, but back then, I had drunk the Kool-Aid in its entirety and believed that my worth in wine hinged on this worthless exam.

Julia and I finished our tasting at 10:30 and drove somewhere for lunch and a bottle of wine. I spent the entire lunch praying for a complete pass. I felt good about the written exam for the first time, but knew that service and tasting were so subjective, I could have gotten tripped up and failed one or both.

At 4 p.m., we went back to the hotel. Each candidate was called by a master sommelier to receive our results in private. Virginia Philip, the master sommelier from The Breakers in Palm Beach as well as a dear mentor and friend, called my name.

"How do you think you did?" she asked.

"I feel really good about it," I said.

"You should," she said. "You passed."

It was the first time in this whole test-taking process that I teared up. I had finally done it. I had passed. Relief took over my entire being.

When I came out of our meeting, everyone was waiting for me. They all knew it was my fourth time and how anxious I had been about the written exam. When I beamed with pride and announced my success, each and every one of them cheered and clapped, even the ones who hadn't been so lucky.

I ran to the bathroom, took off my suit, and put on my jean shorts and a T-shirt with my Croc wedges—the only outfit I felt truly comfortable in. Julia had passed too, and she and I took a cab to the airport.

Dad and Mary Ann were waiting to pick me up when I got home. Stephen was working at On the Square, but I had called him earlier. According to Mary Ann and Dad, he had left the kitchen during service and gone to every table to tell them I had passed.

I'm emotional writing about it because although those years were extremely challenging and stressful, the support from my community was like nothing I could imagine. All of our regulars had been cheering me on, and I had finally given them the results we were all hoping for.

There is no way on earth or in heaven I could have done all of this without incredible help. My mom and Bill, Mary Ann and Dad aka Sweetie and Rushie, and Yia Yia—who would fly down anytime I asked to take care of Cynthia— they were all, of course, a huge part of this team. But I also had a babysitter named Yuridia Cisneros, who was my rock while I was at work.

Yuridia cared for Cynthia for the first two and a half years of her life. She was the one who put her to bed every Thursday, Friday, and Saturday night while I worked. She would stroll her on Main Street, going to visit Nana for me on the days that I couldn't, and dedicated so much time and energy to learning exactly what I wanted for Cynthia and how I wanted things done. When she married and started her own career, she introduced me to Marina Hernandez, the woman who would help me raise both of my children and become what Stephen and I termed our "life coach."

CHAPTER SIXTEEN

Little Stephen

Stephen and I were getting our groove.

We had bought our first house. We were running a restaurant in eastern North Carolina that was garnering excellent press and filling every seat every night we were open. Cynthia was adorable and perfect, and Stephen worshipped her as much as I did. All in all, life seemed exactly as it was supposed to be.

And now, we were going to travel again. We had taken off the first week of December to travel to Thailand for my cousin Dail's wedding. Our love of travel was part of what made us *us*. We both loved seeing new things, having new experiences, and, of course, indulging in the food and drink of the cultures we visited. And now, we rarely took time off work together so that was another reason to be excited.

Our flight left Raleigh-Durham and landed in Chicago, where we changed planes and flew to Tokyo. Once we got to Tokyo, we had an eight-hour layover, allowing us to eat sushi in the cleanest airport known to man before hopping on a shortish flight to Bangkok. After a night in Bangkok, we took a puddle jumper over to the island where the wedding festivities would take place.

On the second day, Dail and his fiancée, Laurie, had rented a boat for everyone to go on a booze cruise—but I barely made my way to the dock before passing out in Stephen's arms.

And I knew. I knew without a doubt.

On the boat, I couldn't drink. I felt completely nauseous and claustrophobic. I didn't say anything to Stephen, I just tried not to think about how angry and betrayed he had felt when he found out about Cynthia.

When we returned to land, I found a small pharmacy and bought a pregnancy test. Just like with Cynthia, almost before the pee hit the wand, a bright pink plus symbol emerged.

My second stop was an internet café, where I emailed Dr. Lee from my personal account asking him if I could make an appointment as soon as I arrived back in the States.

We had six more days left in Thailand, but they felt like six hundred. This was the second time I had felt so sick so far from home—the first time being when I was unknowingly pregnant with Cynthia in New Zealand.

Once I got home, Dr. Lee examined me and confirmed that I would have my second child in early July of 2007.

So much was already happening in 2007: In April, Stephen was scheduled to fly to Anaheim to retake the advanced exam, and my brother and his fiancée were due to marry the same month. And in typical Inie fashion, the bus never stopped. I continued to work, study, and mother Cynthia, while sporting an ever-growing ball in my stomach.

There were some customers who couldn't contain their shock at seeing me opening a bottle of wine at their table with my basketball belly almost touching their shoulder or me walking in high heels to seat them at their table. But another pregnancy wouldn't stop me from doing what I was used to doing, which was working in restaurants, ensuring that each guest's experience was as amazing as possible, and studying wine, preparing to sit for the final Master Sommelier Diploma.

Little Cynthia went with me to get my ultrasound, and when they said it was a boy, no one was as shocked as I was. My mom was one of two girls and I was one of two girls, so naturally, I assumed I would have two girls as well.

Meanwhile, Stephen still couldn't talk to me about this second child—he had thought we were totally done after Cynthia. In fact, he had thought we were done before Cynthia, but as I tell both my children to this day: the only fool-proof contraception is abstinence.

But Nana—no one was as excited as Nana. This would be her first boy, and she could barely hide her enthusiasm. Nana was one of four children, and only one of them was a boy: her brother Bill, whom she loved with her entire heart and spoke of with such admiration and joy. I truly believe my boy was sent to bring her some reconnection with Bill, who had passed away years before.

So, the busy year rolled on. Stephen flew to Anaheim in April and passed the advanced exam in its entirety on his second try. Ken and Elizabeth were married on April 28, and I stood up at the front of the church in a custom-made bridesmaid dress for a seven-month-pregnant woman, looking like I could eat everyone in attendance.

Cynthia and her cousin Shelton were flower girls, and Cynthia had chosen that day to be as ornery as possible, throwing herself on the ground when it was time to be photographed, slamming her fingers down on the organ, and then, of course, picking up all the flower petals she and Shelton and the other flower girl had strewn in the aisle and running them all back to me, standing in the apse of the church. On the third attempt, my Uncle Haywood, who was officiating, indicated to Eleanor, the babysitter hired to take them to the nursery once their duties were done, to grab the girls and usher them upstairs so we could finally start the wedding.

Had I not been seven months pregnant and had it not been my daughter creating the drama, I may have laughed. As it was, the only emotion I could feel was an overwhelming desire to bawl hysterically.

Spring passed, and on the morning of Sunday, July 8, at 4 a.m., I drove myself to the hospital.

Again, I would be induced, but this time, I didn't have to be there at midnight.

My first boyfriend from the fifth grade, Brandon Hale, wheeled my chair up to my room, and by 6 a.m., a nurse had come in and inserted the Pitocin. Burton arrived around 8:30, and Stephen rolled in at 9:45.

I birthed little Stephen like a boss at 11:30 a.m., and Stephen left to play golf.

Two days later, I left the hospital to start our life as a final family of four.

Dr. Lee came in the day I left, right after he circumcised little Stephen, to recommend an IUD.

"The pill," he said sternly, "is clearly not working."

CHAPTER SEVENTEEN

Learning to Mom and Finding Our Forever Home

Little Stephen brought the thunder, the lightning, the rain, and the rainbows.

Never in my life have I known exhaustion and fatigue like I did in little Stephen's first three years. Not only would he not sleep, but he would scream and cry with such a vengeance, I honestly thought he hated me.

How does he even know me to hate me already? I would wonder.

We were living in our two-bedroom house, and his crib was in the same room as Cynthia, almost three years old and sleeping in a twin bed. One morning—on a day when he'd woken up at 3 a.m.—I stood over his crib, rubbing his forehead and softly pleading with him to go to sleep, when Cynthia said to me, "Mom, did we *have* to have him?"

Our family dynamics had changed in a monumental way, and learning to be a mom to two children under three was as hard as anything I had ever done—while at the same time, having two lives so beautifully connected to mine was also magical in every moment.

When I was home, the three of us did everything together, from walking to Nana's for visits to driving to Cotton Valley to see Sweetie and Rushie (the grandparent names for Mary Ann and Dad) to attending church. We all waited patiently for big Stephen to catch up with our unit, and once he did, he became the father he was always destined to be.

When I wasn't home, which was Tuesday to Friday daytimes and Thursday to Saturday nights, Marina mommed for me, and my children loved her as much as they loved Stephen and me. She also helped me learn to relate better to little Stephen. She was a mother of four boys who were almost grown, and she knew just how to be what Stephen needed. From cutting him mangoes she would bring from home to strapping a twin sheet to her back and letting him sleep like the dead while she vacuumed to bringing her grandson to play, Marina helped me better understand little Stephen's needs and wants.

During this time, it became abundantly clear that we were outgrowing our house. Our plan was to build a second floor since the lot would not allow us to grow wider, but first, we would have to get approval from the Town of Tarboro's Historic District Association.

Meanwhile, Stephen and I had befriended a gentleman from King Estate in Oregon at one of the wine dinners we hosted at On the Square, and he had invited us to visit the winery. We had made plans to travel there with Neisy and Stuart Sanderson, the owners of the local bed and breakfast, Main Street Inn, and to leave the kids with Yia Yia, who had now left New York and bought a house a couple of blocks from us.

We flew out in mid-September, and while we were in Texas waiting for our connecting flight home, my dad called and said someone wanted to buy our house.

"What the hell is he talking about?" Stephen asked me.

"Apparently, a woman from Michigan is looking for a one-story house in the historic district, and she loves ours," I told him.

"Well, our house isn't for sale," he said.

"That's what I told Dad, to which he replied, 'Well then, make her an offer she won't accept.'"

Stephen and I had bought that house for a little more than you'd pay for an SUV, and we sold it for almost double what we paid for it, with no counteroffer. Just like that, we returned to Tarboro with thirty-five days to find a new house.

And that is how we found our forever home.

My paternal grandparents, Gran and Papa Bear, built a massive house on South Howard Circle in the late 1950s. One of the first houses built on that street, it was a seven-bedroom house with a hill leading to a pond in the backyard and a tennis court and backboard on the side. When Gran died in 1995, a woman from Tarboro, who now resides in Los Angeles, bought her house and has maintained it ever since.

Beside this house was a modernist home built in 1959 set back from the street, with a horseshoe driveway. Stephen and I had driven by the place a million and one times, always commenting that it might be the ugliest house in Tarboro and maybe the world.

The morning after we had signed the papers agreeing to sell our house on Main Street, I woke up with the strangest thought in my head.

"Stephen!" I nudged him.

He rolled over. "What?" he mumbled.

"I know which house we need to look at today."

Without missing a beat, he muttered, "Is it the ugly one on South Howard Circle?"

Stephen and I have a strange, supernatural power of being able to read each other's thoughts. Normally, it happens with food and drink, but sometimes it goes deeper.

This was one of those times.

We called my dad, who is also a realtor.

"Can we go look at Mr. Raskin's house?" I asked him.

"Great idea," he said. "I'll pick you up in thirty."

The second Dad opened the front door, my breath stopped.

Directly in front of me were three massive windows overlooking the same backyard I had seen as a child every time I went to Gran and Papa Bear's. The light from these floor-to-ceiling windows filled the entire house, and in turn, lit up anyone standing in the living room. The basement had a game room and a wet bar, with 1970s green-and-yellow-patterned wallpaper in the dining room.

With no doubts whatsoever, I said to Stephen, "This is the house I want. This is the house for us."

He nodded. We both knew instantaneously.

At that point, the Raskin house had been on the market for three and a half years, and the going price was $200,000.

"We can't afford it," I told Dad.

"You don't know until you make an offer."

My entire family was dying for us to move out of our house on Main. We were cramped in there, and by this time, big Stephen had claimed the couch, and the kids and I were sleeping in my bed pretty much every night.

Nana called me before I had even walked in the door at On the Square to tell me she wanted to help Stephen and me with the down payment for our new house.

We graciously accepted her offer, and with that money and the sale of our house, we offered Mr. Raskin $150,000 for this house he had built and maintained for so long. It was $50,000 less than he was asking for, and $150,000 less than the original asking price, three years earlier.

Before long, my dad called and said Mr. Raskin had agreed to sell his house at that price.

"You're kidding me!" I screamed. "Does it always happen like this?"

"It *never* happens like this," my dad said.

We closed on our old house on October 30, 2009, and on the new one on October 31 and moved in that afternoon with a million hands on deck, including Marina, On the Square employees, and, of course, my entire family.

Now, not only did little Stephen and Cynthia have their own rooms, but we also had a guest room for when Stephen's dad, Pop Pop, visited from upstate New York.

And so, in late fall of 2009—when Cynthia was beginning pre-K at Princeville Montessori and Stephen had just turned two—we found ourselves living in our forever home.

I was in love with the house and was so grateful for Mr. Raskin's generosity in selling it at a fraction of the original price that I took him a homemade caramel cake along with a thank-you letter. He wrote me back saying how much Gran's neighborly kindness had meant to him.

Less than a month after we closed, he died of cancer. He was survived by his wife and three children. When I think about how everything played out and how much I adore this house that he also adored, it's very clear to me that timing is everything and the universe is always working in ways we can never truly comprehend.

CHAPTER EIGHTEEN

Coming Home to Jesus

After 9/11, I stopped talking to God. All I could feel was my anger that so many people had died under Her or His watch. I stopped going to church, and I stopped praying.

But all that changed when Cynthia was born on September 12, 2004.

I started reaching out to God and praying for the hurting people, and of course, for strength and wisdom when it came to raising my two young babies.

Not long after that, I had a true homecoming with Jesus, partly in thanks to our young minister and his wife, who had become dear friends, and partly because of Mary Ann inviting me to attend a weekly women's Bible study with her at our church.

Howard Memorial Presbyterian Church was the church where I was baptized, where my father was baptized, and where my paternal grandfather was baptized. Now, both of my children and my brother's and sister's children have been baptized there too. Which is to say: My family has a long history with Howard Memorial.

Within years of being back in Tarboro, I was actively involved in the church. When my children were little, I helped lead Vacation Bible School and even chaperoned our youth group on a mission trip to New York. Then in 2010, I was elected an elder. I'm pretty sure I was the first elder our church ever elected who was married to an agnostic.

But my children weren't always thrilled about going to church—and I have the stories to prove it. When they were young, the church would hold an annual talent show that lasted about ninety minutes—about eighty-five minutes too long for my son, whose least favorite pastime was sitting still and listening.

One particular year, the talent was much older—so old you could have called it a senior citizen talent show—and one gentleman had signed up for at least six spots, each one a poetry reading, not one of which lasted less than five minutes.

Baby Stephen, as we called him back then, was fidgety and fussy and downright mad that we were there, and when Mr. Haislip marched back on the stage for the third time, Stephen looked at me and loudly sighed, "Not again."

"Hush," I whispered back.

From a husband and wife duet of "Joyful, Joyful, We Adore Thee" to a painting display from a local artist, for my son, this was the talent show that would never end.

Until . . .

Until Dr. Winslow slowly and intentionally walked onto the stage in khaki slacks, a long-sleeved T-shirt, and a fisherman's vest. With him, he brought a large exercise ball and a handmade recorder.

Stephen stopped rocking in his seat and watched Dr. Winslow with great anticipation and expectation.

Dr. Winslow centered the exercise ball on the stage and gracefully and carefully sat cross-legged on it.

The room was silent as he lifted the recorder to his lips and started playing "Stairway to Heaven."

Baby Stephen leaned over to me and whispered in my ear, "Now *that* is talent."

There were also more experiences than I can count of the church as a place that anchored and held our family in community and love of Jesus. One December, my dad, Kate, and I were asked to reflect on Christmas as part of the family advent season. I wrote the following to read at our Sunday church service:

For unto us a child is born. Shazam!

In the fifth grade, I made my true acting debut as Gladys Herdman in The Best Christmas Pageant Ever. *I spent that December traveling from school to school around the county, entertaining the masses with a cast of other children. It was a fun year, and I will always remember being very excited to play Herdman.*

My father used to read The Best Christmas Pageant Ever *to us each and every season, and it was a very real way to get us prepared for the holidays. I was obsessed with the Herdmans and loved the fact they were always in endless trouble.*

My childhood was very similar to my life now: It consisted of my family and me running around like chickens with our heads chopped off. At Christmastime, we were even more frantic. We spent most of December going to church on Sundays, preparing for Christmas parties, buying gifts for family and friends, and waiting impatiently for Christmas Eve.

The music is a very big part of Christmas for me. I love to hear "What Child Is This?" sung by our church choir. Papa Bear would beg to hear "Mary's Little Boy Child" sung by Sheila and Sheila only. When I would get to church on Sundays in December, I would immediately look in the bulletin to see which Christmas carols we would sing. Even as I write this, I am listening to Louis Armstrong's "Walking in a

Winter Wonderland," and before this, it was "O Holy Night," "O Come All Ye Faithful," "God Rest Ye Merry Gentlemen," "Hark! The Herald Angels Sing"—I am that girl. That girl who can listen to Christmas music twenty-four-seven from December 1ˢᵗ until the 31ˢᵗ and be perfectly content. I love the music that comes with Christmas, and I love it the most when I hear it at Howard Memorial Presbyterian Church, sung by our choir and congregation. It just isn't Christmas for me if I don't have the music.

'Twas the night before Christmas and all through the house . . .

I don't want to take away from Kate's Christmas, but on Christmas Eve, everything calmed down for a moment. We would finish delivering last-minute gifts and go see the grandparents: first Nana, then Gran. Nana would have tipsy cake—the best tipsy cake ever—and Gran's house would be decorated with three different Christmas trees and the coolest candle fans that spun angels. Someone (we're not sure who) would be down the hill with a red light, and the cousins would run to the window to see Rudolph outside. Make no mistake, I am going to do that for my children this Christmas Eve.

After the eight o'clock service, we would go home and get ready for bed. Right up until our mid-twenties, when we started to get married, we would make pallets on Kate's bedroom floor (the only time of year we were allowed to go into Kate's room) and get ready for bed. Silent night, holy night. *We would lie on the floor in the dark and wait, not falling asleep until morning.* All is calm. Peace on Earth. *That was real Christmas for me: lying on the floor with Kate, Burton, and Ken, with no fighting or fussing, only sweet anticipation of Christmas Day.*

It came without ribbons. It came without tags. It came without packages, boxes, or bags.

In December of 2000, I worked in Manhattan on Christmas Eve, and when I left work at 10 p.m., I took the subway to Penn Station and got on a train to Long Island, alone, to stay with a friend's family. There weren't many people on the train, so I had an hour to sit quietly and reflect on the past year and what this holiday was bringing. I had spoken to Mary Ann earlier in the day, and she told me to go into my favorite store, Banana Republic, and buy the long, black coat I wanted as an early Christmas present from her. I did, and I was wearing that coat on the train, wondering what she, Dad,

Nana, Mom, Burton, Kate, and Ken were do-ing. I wondered how Burton's solo sounded. I wondered if Dad was going to slice oranges the next morning and keep them refrigerated, just the way I liked them.

That December, I really didn't have much of a Christmas. We didn't have a tree in our Brooklyn townhouse. I worked every day and ev-ery night and didn't do any shopping. I didn't go to church at all, and the only Christmas music I really heard was the Muzak in the elevator. I spent Christmas Eve with someone else's family, and as sweet as they were, on Christmas morn-ing, the only thing I wanted was to call home.

When I did, Burton answered the phone, and I remember her saying, "Inie, I have the best Christmas present for you. Are you ready? They're building a Bojangles across from the Walmart. Merry Christmas!" As you can imagine, nothing could have made me laugh more. And then, in true, Burton fashion, in perfect pitch, she sang me her solo from church the night before.

I'll be home for Christmas.

Christmas isn't Christmas for me unless I'm in Tarboro. Fortunately, I discovered that sooner rather than later, and I look forward to making

Christmas for my husband and my children as perfect as mine always were. Reading from The Greatest Christmas Pageant Ever, *going to church and listening to the sounds of the season, participating in advent, breakfast with Mary and Joseph, and finding peace on Christmas Eve . . .*

CHAPTER NINETEEN

Laughter Break! Chocolate by the Bald Man Syringe

In January of 2009, when Little Stephen was eighteen months and Cynthia was four years old, Stephen and I drove with them to upstate New York to visit Stephen's father, Pop Pop. Pop Pop lives in a small cabin at the top of a hill in Lordville, a hamlet of seventy-eight people on the Delaware River, on the New York-Pennsylvania border. From then on, we would visit Pop Pop every winter and every summer—a getaway from the bustling restaurant.

I absolutely love it in Lordville, especially in the summer. An entire week in this secluded part of the world renews my faith in humanity and fills me with the kind of inner peace that can only come from time spent alone in nature.

In the summer of 2010, as part of our visit to Pop Pop's cabin, we decided to make an overnight trip to Manhattan to see friends and eat at Union Square Cafe, one of New York's favorite restaurants, which somehow we had never tried, even when we lived there.

We were staying with Stephen's childhood friend John Petrizzo and his wife, Lisa Leingang. Lisa was in California working at the time, so Stephen and I were going to sleep on the pullout couch while the two kids slept on a floor mattress in the spare bedroom.

Weeks before, I had contacted my friend Maggie to recommend a babysitter for the kids when we went out to dinner, and she had put me in touch with a woman named Emily who, when I called her, said she would like to interview me about my children before she decided to babysit them. Her sophisticated British accent was intimidating, but not nearly as intimidating as the price she quoted: $28/hour to keep both children.

I was less than thrilled about spending $140 before even opening a menu, but I caved, knowing that finding such a quality babysitter for less in the city was most likely not an option.

We set off from Tarboro on a late June Wednesday and drove as far north as we could, making it to somewhere around south Jersey before stopping at a dumpy motel, just so we could all sleep in a bed and not have to drive any longer.

I would always read a book aloud to the family while Stephen drove, and on this particular journey, I was reading *The Miraculous Adventure of Edward Tulane* by Kate

DiCamillo. It was so riveting that Stephen refused to pull over for us to use the restroom because he didn't want me to stop reading. The kids loved it just as much, and although my voice was so exhausted I could barely talk by the time we got to Jersey, our hearts had been transformed by this china rabbit beloved by his owner.

When I wasn't reading to the kids, I would tell them stories of Candy Land, with them starring as the main characters. Every day, they would beg me to tell them these stories of chocolate rivers, marshmallow rafts, and flowers filled with ring pops. Little did I know that pretty soon, I would be starring in my own kind of Candy Land.

After sleeping in the motel, we parked the car in Cranford and took the train into Manhattan. I took extra care in telling the Candy Land story that day to build excitement about our first stop in New York, Max Brenner: Chocolate by the Bald Man. The Willy Wonka's chocolate factory of restaurants.

Stephen and Cynthia were so excited they could barely contain themselves, and the closer the train got to the station, the more jittery they became. As you might imagine, they must have asked "when will we be there?" at least a hundred times. At last, we got to Penn Station and jumped on a subway to Union Square, where there was barely a three-minute walk to the restaurant, even with toddlers.

It was slammed. I mean, completely and totally filled to capacity. And wouldn't you know it, there was a forty-five-minute wait at 11:30 on a Thursday morning.

Those forty-five minutes were plenty of time for Cynthia to bear witness to a chocolate syringe that she decided in the span of one millisecond that she absolutely had to have.

"That's what I want," she said to me.

"Okay, baby, we just have to wait until we're seated. It'll be a little while, just be patient."

If she said she wanted that chocolate syringe once, she said it a million times, and by the time the host seated us at a four-top sandwiched between two other four-tops, I thought I was going to lose my entire suitcase of shits.

Did I mention we went to the restaurant with our luggage?

That's how we rolled then.

Before the server brought our water, Cynthia repeated, "I want that chocolate syringe, Mama." Stephen glared at me as if to say he couldn't take it any longer. I glared back as if to say, "No shit, Sherlock, it's my name she keeps saying at the end of each sentence."

The server came over to deliver our water, and Cynthia looked up at her and politely said, "I would like the chocolate syringe, please."

The woman looked surprised but delighted that she could go ahead and get our order, so that the table could be turned quickly for all the other tourists/suckers waiting to dine. Getting in and out quickly was fine by us—we were only there for dessert. Stephen and I had reservations at a sushi place for lunch, but we knew our chances of the children behaving at a sit-down restaurant were much higher if we bribed them with chocolate beforehand.

I decided on the chocolate fondue for little Stephen, and while we waited impatiently for our desserts, Cynthia talked incessantly about the chocolate syringe.

I have never been so grateful for a food order to arrive in my entire life.

Little Stephen and I were on one side of the table, our backs against the chair backs of a table that sounded like they were speaking Italian. Cynthia and big Stephen sat across from us, with their backs to the server station. I was helping little Stephen skewer pound cake and marshmallows to dip into the chocolate while independent Cynthia focused on getting her syringe to shoot chocolate in her mouth.

"I can't get it, Dad, it won't come out. Why is it not working?"

Big Stephen took the syringe from her and inspected it, trying to find out what, if anything, was keeping melted chocolate locked into the syringe. He fiddled with it for about a minute before aiming it at my forehead and pressing on the plunger flange—the piece you push on a syringe to inject the serum.

Without warning—before I could even think about telling him why aiming a chocolate syringe at his wife's face was a terrible idea—what seemed like liters of chocolate came flying out, hitting me in my hair, all over my face, and on the shoulders of my white eyelet dress. The chocolate literally drenched me, but while I quickly thanked God that I didn't believe in concealed carry, I looked at Stephen to find he wasn't even looking at me. He was staring at the table of

Italians behind us, who had also been hit by the chocolate and were absolutely livid.

He jumped up to tell them how sorry he was, and in my utter confusion, I turned around to ask him what in the hell he was doing. When they saw my face, they realized the real damage had happened to me, not them.

Horrified by the fury on my face, they shooed him away, saying in broken English, "Just go take care of your hostile wife."

I was too mad to speak, and I left the table for the bathroom to try to get myself cleaned up. It was of no use. Eventually, we made it to John and Lisa's apartment on Irving to get settled and for me to take a hot shower before going to dinner. Sometime around 5:30 p.m., the buzzer rang indicating that Emily, the $28/hour babysitter had arrived.

Stephen, who was almost three at the time, stayed upstairs in the apartment with big Stephen and John while Cynthia, always the curious child, walked downstairs to the lobby to greet Emily and let her into the building.

As soon as I reached the glass doors on the ground level and saw Emily outside, I inhaled a deep, long breath.

British Emily, who I was getting ready to pay more an hour than anyone I had ever paid in my life, had royal blue hair, multiple face piercings, and all you could see on her arms and neck were sleeves of tattoos.

Oh God, I thought, *I'm not sure little Stephen is going to be able to handle this.*

Let me paint you a picture of Tarboro in 2010. We had black people; we had white people; we had Hispanic people.

We had intimate relationships with people of all of these three backgrounds. At the time, no one in our friend group looked like Emily. Yes, my sister Burton has multiple tattoos, but most of them were hidden by clothes. This was going to be fun.

I opened the door, greeted Emily, who greeted me back with lovely manners and the most gorgeous British accent.

Cynthia looked up at her without missing a beat and said, "I really like your blue hair."

Emily thanked her, and we made our way up to the third floor to John's apartment.

Thank God Stephen and John were ready to walk out the door.

As soon as little Stephen saw Emily, he shrieked with pure terror and started wailing so loudly that people in the neighboring apartments opened their doors to make sure child abuse wasn't occurring.

Emily gave me the thumbs up that she was in control, and big Stephen, John, and I bolted out of there with fierce determination.

We hopped into a cab, and as we were driving toward Union Square, I told them I needed to go back—I couldn't leave little Stephen hysterical like that.

Stephen took my hand, looked me in the eye, and said, "Inez, you're being a little judgmental, don't you think? As a Jesus follower, you need to relax, have a little faith, and enjoy tonight with no kids."

And that, my friends, is all it took.

CHAPTER TWENTY

Youth of On the Square

The Burroughs family came into our lives before Stephen and I had even married one another.

Xavyer, the second oldest of four children, walked into the restaurant sometime in early 2003 and said Dr. Richards had sent him to help us wash dishes.

Dr. Richards was my dad's partner in buying On the Square and one of the kindest, most unassuming gentlemen you could hope to meet. Apparently, he had mentioned to Stephen that he volunteered as a wrestling coach for the high school, and one of the kids, a sophomore, needed a job and would be a great addition to our nighttime team of three.

In typical Stephen fashion, he had failed to tell me anything of this, so when Xavyer came through the door, head down, timid, and quietly whispering that he was there to wash dishes, I had no idea what he was talking about. I told him there must be some confusion, but when I ran back to the kitchen to check, Stephen said, "Yes, he's here to wash dishes. Dr. Richards recommends him."

Back in the dining room, I found an even more frightened Xavyer. I apologized for not knowing he was coming, and we got him situated with an apron and gloves, and he started washing dishes.

Xavyer was unlike any high schooler I had ever met. He was quiet, meek, and focused. He had dreams of attending NC State to become an engineer, and he was on track to get there, holding steady at second in his class and now holding down a part-time job to help pay for his education. He didn't smile often, but when he did, it was blinding, and his deep voice was mesmerizing.

Within just a few short weeks, Stephen and I came to love and respect him and rely on him in the kitchen. I'll never forget his brothers, sister, and mom coming in for dinner one Thursday evening and Jasmine, the youngest child, ordering the cheese plate. I was concerned that she wouldn't enjoy it or understand it, since our cheeses weren't like anything you could buy locally—they were all funky cheeses, shipped in from Di Bruno Brothers in Philadelphia. But the child ate every single bite of it. In fact, the whole family finished their meals, leaving nothing on the plate. We would soon learn that the Burroughs family did not waste food. They ate what was on their plates, and they would happily finish yours if you offered it. Xavyer would rarely talk, which could make conversations difficult, but on the rare occasions he let his guard down, it was quite evident he was amused at Stephen's sarcasm and my impatience for carelessness. We started to rely on him as part of our small team.

Meanwhile, other young people were applying to work at On the Square as well. The children I had spent my entire young adulthood babysitting, Horton and Eleanor Redhage, were now in high school, and they worked in the kitchen and in the front of the house, respectively. Before I knew it, we had created an incredible team of young people: high schoolers, college students, nurses, teachers, and even those who wanted On the Square to be their full-time gig. While not as diverse as Windows, it was still quite a diverse front-of-house team, with Xavyer and later Jasmine Burroughs highlighting our African American community and Eliseo Hernandez representing our Hispanic community.

And boy, did we work hard and have fun. Back in my day, I was manic about service, and I had very little patience for sloppy mistakes. If you liked my approach, we were golden, but if you didn't—well, those were the people who soon quit, saying waiting tables wasn't their cup of tea.

Meanwhile, Stephen led a team of young people in the kitchen with very little turnover. And with the exception of one person who had a culinary degree, the rest of the kitchen staff were young people with zero professional kitchen experience.

I didn't know it then, but what we were able to create at that restaurant was nothing short of extraordinary. Taking mostly people who had grown up in Edgecombe County and teaching them how to cook, describe, and eloquently serve dishes to a clientele—some of whom were well-traveled and well-versed in food and some of whom weren't—made our restaurant unique. Not to mention the fact that our wine list was unlike anything North Carolina had ever seen in terms of its eclectic variety and its unheard-of pricing. Thanks to all this, On the Square quickly became one of the hottest restaurants in our state, attracting customers from all over the Eastern Seaboard.

Over the years, we encouraged and mentored many aspiring chefs and even one professional wine buyer—our dear Xavyer. Yes: Our first OTS team member is now a head buyer for Millesima on the Upper East Side in Manhattan. After starting out washing dishes in 2003, he quickly moved up to working the cold station and then, by his junior year, to the grill. In the fall of his senior year, he became our runner in the dining room, and when he turned eighteen that March, he became a server. He worked as a server the entire summer before leaving for North Carolina State University. One of our regular customers who loved Xavyer gave him a laptop as his graduation present. I will never forget the expression on his face when they gave it to him—he was in utter disbelief, combined with the greatest smile you've ever seen.

While Xavyer was living in Raleigh for college, we kept in touch, and I would visit him when my brother's band played on Hillsborough Street. At that time, I was also consulting on a new wine-themed restaurant in Raleigh, and the chef hired him as a server on the spot. Unfortunately, the restaurant didn't last long, and one day when Xavyer arrived at work, the doors were locked.

Throughout his entire tenure in college, he would work at On the Square whenever he came home for a break as well as during the summer, and when he turned twenty-one, he expressed an interest in working the floor as a sommelier.

It was a dream come true to pass the wine torch to Xavyer, and On the Square quickly enrolled him in the Court of Master Sommeliers Introductory Course held at the Angus Barn, where he passed the exam in June 2011—the same year I wrote the court telling them I was no longer interested in becoming a Master after failing for the fourth time.

Xavyer was a natural when it came to talking about wine, and he exuded passion for the grape in every circle of every tasting we attended. Eventually, my dear friend Max Kast— who was also my dedicated study partner for the last leg of my Master Sommelier journey—asked me if he could hire Xavyer to work for him at Fearrington Village. Knowing it would be incredibly selfish to hold Xavyer back living in Tarboro, I gave Max my blessing to reach out to Xavyer.

From there, Xavyer was on a roll. After working at Fearrington for a couple of years, he went to Houston to run the wine program at a steakhouse. And now he's landed at Millesima, where he is a lead buyer for the company.

In March of 2020, several days before our country went into the pandemic lockdown, I met Xavyer in Manhattan to work La Paulée, an extravagant wine weekend where vintners from Burgundy are the celebrities of the event. In addition to the current offerings of these wineries, collectors from all over the world attend the Saturday night dinner, bringing ultra-rare bottles from their cellars to be opened by a team of sommeliers touted to be the ultimate wine professionals in the country. One must be invited to work this prestigious event, and because of my friendship with David Gordon, one of the wine consultants for the Borgata who hired me, I have been working La Paulée for a number of years. David also accepted my gentle nudging to invite Xavyer into this exclusive mix, and because David loves me so very much, he extended Xavyer an invitation.

To see Xavyer in action serving wines that most sommeliers dream of tasting brings me a sense of joy that comes only with the passing of time and being able to be here for it. Xavyer came to On the Square as a determined sophomore in high school who dreamed of becoming an engineer. Through working in hospitality in a small town in rural eastern North Carolina where wine was a focus, he found purpose and energy around an art that incorporates geography, science, history, and the senses. What is more is that he has taken a similar path to me in that he lives in Manhattan where he is afforded all of the opportunities a sommelier could want in terms of exposure to wines. When he and I text, I am overcome with pride, admiration, and love for this young man who has found a deep passion for wine. On November 12, 2020, he texted me a photograph of a bottle of Domaine de La Romanée-Conti Montrachet 2017—a bottle of white Burgundy made from a grand cru site by one of the most well-regarded vintners. His text below read: "Hi Inez!! I got some pretty cool white wine as an aperitif for pizza (wink emoji)! I hope everything is working out well for you guys in tha 'boro! We'll probably enter another lockdown soon, so I'm trying to enjoy my freedom while I still have it. I remember my first bottle of wine was the Nora Albariño I had at the bar at OTS. Quite the journey it's been from there, lol. Thank you and Stephen for everything! —X"

Quite the journey it has been, my sweet and beautiful Xavyer. Quite the journey.

CHAPTER TWENTY-ONE

Leaving the Path of the Master Sommelier

T he first two years of Stephen's life were not simple. It would be easy to blame him for being a difficult baby, but as I reflect, I know the truth: I was a difficult mama.

His first eight months were shared with wine books and study questions as I geared up to take the Master Sommelier exam for the first time. I remember watching him sleep in his crib while I tried to memorize the four yeasts used in sherry production. Baby Stephen, as I named him, often cried in frustration during those months, maybe in hopes I would leave the wine notes to spend more time enjoying his babyhood.

But not to be distracted or deterred from my path of becoming a Master Sommelier, I muffled his cries with frustrated sighs of my own.

A child requires nourishment, of course, but a happy child also requires love and attention. If you don't give enough in either of these areas, they'll be sure to let you know.

A child doesn't complicate your life. A child makes you come to immediate grips with what you need to change in your life—and in my case, the child was right on about what needed to stay and what needed to go.

In 2011, I took my fourth attempt at the Master Sommelier exam. By this time, I had been trying to pass the exam for three years.

I had gone to Sonoma in January of 2008 to take it for the first time and passed no portion of it. Then Stephen and I had gone to Cincinnati in the summer of 2009 to take it together, and I had passed the theory portion only. For the Masters, the theory test is oral as opposed to the written version you take for the advanced test. After this first attempt for Stephen, he said screw it—he had no interest in pursuing a title that was going to change nothing about his life or his pay.

But I carried on, trying and failing a third time in February 2010, not long after we moved into our forever home. I traveled to Napa and didn't pass service or tasting. For the Masters exam, you have three years to pass all three parts. This meant that, having gotten no further passes in 2010, if I didn't pass both tasting and service when I went again in 2011, I would lose my theory portion and have to "reset."

When I came home from Dallas that Sunday in 2011, having passed no further portions, I said goodbye to the program with a letter to the court and a good cry to my husband.

My exact words were:

Dear Court of Master Sommeliers:

If I am reading this letter aloud, then congratulations to me. I have passed the rigorous and grueling Master Sommelier exam, and I now can gloriously add the initials M.S. next to my name.

If, however, I am not reading this letter aloud, and you are, in fact, reading it to yourselves, then I have not been so successful in my venture.

As they say in the movies, "It's been a long time."

So, let's start, shall we? Let's start at the very beginning, a very good place to start . . .

Some of you may remember August of 2000 when the Introductory Course was taught at the CIA at Greystone in Napa. I was one of the people attending, and I listened intently to the lessons taught by Damon Ornowski, Robert Bath, and Evan Goldstein. At 24 years old, I thought I had gone to heaven listening to wine speak and learning about this fascinating, hedo-nistic beverage.

My seat mates were John & Ellen Hunt of Napa, and Ellen Hunt was working at Rudd Estates, a new winery that was just getting ready to release its first vintage. David Ramey was the wine-maker, and Damon Ornowski, our instructor, was also working in the winery.

As all of you know, the Court of Master Sommeliers is as much about relationships as it is about knowing what is in a Tom & Jerry cocktail.

During my introductory course, I became fast friends with Ellen & John, and not only did our fast friendship land me a tour of Rudd Winery, but it also landed a prime seat at a launch party luncheon at Jean Georges' Nougatine Room in Manhattan later that month.

Had I arrived, or what?

I can honestly say when I left Napa to go back to New York, three months into my job as Beverage Manager at Windows on the World, I came back a much more confident and able wine professional.

If there is anything the Court masters, it is instilling professionalism and confidence in each candidate who comes into their reach.

I went back to Windows proud of my accomplishment and eager to continue my studies in the vast, never-ending world of wine.

Andrea Immer Robinson, Master Sommelier, and inspiration for my job application at Windows, set up blind tastings for Patrick Bickford (then of Jean Georges) and Karen King (then of Union Square Cafe). I listened intently as I watched her show how Pinot Grigio can sometimes have a pinkish tinge and Shiraz is almost always opaque.

The more I learned about wine, the more I wanted to know, and with Andrea's consent, I signed up to take the Advanced Certification in October 2001.

She told me to read Sotheby's from cover to cover, and then, she said, I would be fine for theory.

I'm not sure what I did wrong, but 9/11 or no 9/11, I would not have passed the advanced.

I remember the phone call from Master Sommelier Bob Bath telling me I could opt out of the exam if I felt like I needed to, but I said no, I wanted something to take my mind off of all that was happening in the world.

Also, with no job, what could be a better time?

Stephen & I rented a pick-up truck and drove cross-country to San Francisco, where the exam was being held at the Hotel Monaco. I'll never forget getting into that room approximately 15 minutes after the class had started.

It was a week to be remembered, and the Thursday night before the last exam was October 11, where restaurants all over the US donated proceeds to Windows of Hope.

We ate at the Slanted Door in the old location, and our rental truck was towed because we followed the crowd and parked in the middle of the street.

We got the car from the police department around 2 in the morning, and I took the service examination in a total fog, failing it miserably, to say the least.

One memorable moment was Jay Fletcher asking me for a cocktail made with Bourbon, and I responded with a Jack & Coke. When he asked me the measures for the cocktail, I said, "I make mine half & half."

The fact the Court let me come back is a testament to their good will.

I took 2002 off, traveled to France to work the harvest in Morey St. Denis, moved back to my hometown and opened a restaurant and wine store with my fiancé.

The year 2003 started out with a bang—a marriage and a new job. The day after my wedding, I left North Carolina for New Jersey to begin my stint as wine director at the Borgata Hotel Casino & Spa.

We opened in July, and I made arrangements to go back to San Francisco in October to retake the advanced.

Second time staying at Hotel Monaco, and the memories of seeing Brian Julyan in his gym shorts in the business center has stayed with me forever.

Again, a great experience, and this time, I passed service and tasting, losing to theory again, but not leaving San Francisco without more knowledge, more friends, and more drive to get through the Master Sommelier program.

I went back to Borgata still feeling confident because I had a spent a solid week absorbing wine, spirits, and what it means to "take care of a guest."

I will never forget the CEO of Borgata telling me, when I do pass, it will be that much sweeter. Oh, how right he was.

We have to skip 2004 because that is when I gave birth to my precious daughter, Cynthia, who will probably breeze through the MS program at the young age of 22 and then move on to Africa to work in the Peace Corps.

I tried again in 2005 in New York City, and when Master Sommelier Greg Harrington called me on the phone to tell me I hadn't passed theory yet again, I wasn't surprised or heartbroken. Life was different, and I wasn't prepared.

However, when 2006 started, I was on the warpath, and I was going to do whatever it took to pass the advanced, even if it meant I had to stop drinking only so I could study more.

Things went as planned, and when Virginia Philip came to get me in Cincinnati to tell me I had passed, I cried big, fat tears of joy. It was such a memorable moment, and I don't think I have ever felt prouder of not giving up.

Fortunately, 2007 was the year to take off before sitting for the Masters, and I decided to have a son then, just so I wouldn't mess up my path for sommelier stardom.

It worked out well, and in February 2008, I traveled to Sonoma to watch Emily Wines receive the Krug Cup.

I didn't pass any part on my first try, but it was an experience to learn from, and I truly learned what was expected and how to go about making my way to becoming a master member of the Court.

I spent the rest of 2008 and all of 2009 studying. Practicing. Tasting. In fact, I traveled to New York to compete in the Best Sommelier in America competition where I was recognized as second runner-up. San Francisco, Chicago, and Tarboro. What a moment. Again, there is no way I could have even competed without the lessons I learned through the Court.

It paid off in theory because Virginia gave me the good news of accomplishing one section of the exam when I re-sat in July of 2009. Ironically, it was theory, the section that took me four times to pass in the advanced.

The next year came all too quickly, and I have to say when I didn't pass service, it hurt. It almost hurt enough to say, I give up, I'm done, no more torture, no more time away from my family who has already sacrificed enough. As my daughter vehemently told me, "I hate wine because it takes you far away all of the time."

But La Paulée happened less than a month later, and when my service was so appreciated by the gentlemen at my table, they actually tipped me, I knew who I had to thank for that.

While the Court hadn't deemed my service good enough to pass, it had instilled in me what it means to give the best possible service and take care of the guest.

I left San Francisco prouder than ever to have been recognized for great service.

April brought the Top Somm competition in Palm Beach, and blessings abound, I won. Both of these moments brought me out of the slumps, and as they say, "God doesn't shut one door without opening another."

The year 2010 also brought about something else very special. In fact, even more special than being tipped for great service or winning a competition. It brought about a friendship, a special wine-related friendship that I wouldn't trade the world for.

Max Kast, Beverage Director at Fearrington House, and I started studying together as well as meeting to blind taste.

Master Sommelier Tim Gaiser, who so generously gave his time when visiting his daughter Maria in Chapel Hill, was a big part of starting the friendship.

Each visit to Chapel Hill was hosted by Max at Fearrington as Tim gave us valuable feedback on how to taste deductively and correctly. Thanks to Tim's time and talents, my tasting improved 100-fold.

Max and I continued to meet and email, and my first real wine friendship in North Carolina began, my husband not included.

Max has been instrumental in my goal of obtaining the Master Sommelier pin. We text, email, taste, and listen, and without him, I wouldn't have been able to survive this past week.

There is no doubt in my mind, he will be a Master Sommelier and maybe a Master of Wine as well.

Exam time was quickly approaching, and again, the generosity of good souls came into play when Master Sommelier Matt Citriglia invited and allowed me to come to Columbus, Ohio, to do the mac-daddy of tasting regimens. Completely and totally beyond what anyone has ever hosted in terms of nose, palate, and site, it was truly a boot camp. Spirits, fortified, high acid, low alcohol, inorganic earth, you name it, we had a chance to break it down. No charge, and the experience was priceless. Another lesson in the Court of Master Sommeliers. You guys (y'all) really want us to pass!

Saturday, February 5, I arrived in San Jose at Master Sommelier Eric Entrikin's house to taste two flights of six back-to-back. The next morning, I drove north to San Francisco to blind taste with Tim and the wonderful Emily Wines. On a Sunday . . . Superbowl Sunday, to be precise.

Eric had invited me to stay with him during my 3 days, and when I came back from San Francisco that Superbowl Sunday afternoon, he had poured four red wines. Brunello, Rioja Reserva, Left Bank Bordeaux and Châteauneuf-du-Pape. They were lined up next to one another just to show me and teach me the difference between stewed fruits, dried fruits, fresh fruits, and baked fruits. It was incredible.

Again, the generosity of the Court in unimaginable amounts.

I flew to Dallas to take tasting and service. I was more nervous about tasting, but what could I do? The clock was ticking. This was my chance to shine. If I didn't pass this time, my theory gets taken away.

Tasting went okay; I wasn't sure of my technique or my time. I am normally a speed taster, and this, unfortunately, was not a speed tasting.

Service was a whole different story, and while, I truly believe my technique was passing, I'm not sure my stiffness gave me a pass. In fact, when I got to my final table to be asked a math question I was completely unprepared for, I gave my answer based on prayer alone.

"You own a restaurant, right?"

"Yes sir," I say.

"How much of your restaurant business do you do on prayer?"

"You'd be surprised," was my response.

That was the end of service.

I left. I cried. I beat myself up for not being able to give the best, fluid answer there is.

I felt defeated.

And that is why . . .

I'm done. I am worn out. I can't play anymore.

I have everything I need to be a wonderfully excellent, professional sommelier. In fact, I have enough to run a successful restaurant. I have enough to have two children and a husband who love me no matter what I pass or don't pass.

Almost 11 years later, my ride is ending. It is ending because I am truly happy with what I have and who I have become.

I thank the Court for being a major part of my wine route. I would not be where I am without you.

With sincere gratitude,
Inez Holderness Ribustello

The minute I sent that letter, I believe my wine career and my emotional health reached another plane. I went back to loving wine rather than worrying about it, and I finally found myself in a place where I could soar as a parent and a wife—a place where everything was harmonized and in balance. When I woke up the next morning, I felt a feeling I can't describe, a high that reached the heavens, a relief that kept relieving.

Of course, it was tough telling people over and over again that I hadn't passed, but even that didn't take away from the relief I felt after deciding to stop trying. It felt amazing. My family had supported me through each and every one of my attempts, and they were even more supportive when I told them I wasn't going back.

Not long after writing my letter to the Court of Master Sommeliers, I got home from work and sat on the couch to enjoy a glass of bubbly before crashing in bed. As per usual, Baby Stephen woke up and ran into the living room, crying about a bad dream.

He sat on my lap while I stroked his hair and watched him calm down in my arms.

About two minutes later, Cynthia, having heard his cries, ran out to join us.

A year earlier, my other hand would have been on my laptop, and I would have been trying to memorize the aging requirements of Franciacorta Satèn. But that night, my left hand was free to take Cynthia into my lap and love on them both at the same time.

I wasn't giving up; I wasn't giving in.

I was just giving more.

More to those who really deserve my time and energy.

My son turning four helped me see that very clearly.

My interaction with Cynthia after the exam:

"Did you win, Mama?"

"No, baby, I didn't."

Quiet. No comments. No reaction.

"I'm sorry, honey, I didn't win."

No comment. No reaction. No nothing.

I say it again. "I'm sorry, honey, I didn't pass. I didn't do it. I lost."

Again, no comment. No reaction.

I look in the backseat.

My Cynthia, my daughter. My miracle child born on September 12.

She's in the backseat looking at a piece of plastic she's found on the floor.

"Did you hear me, honey?"

No response.

"Did you hear me?" I say again.

She looks up at me with the biggest smile I've ever seen.

"I'm so glad you're home," she says.

It is worth noting that in October of 2018, the Court of Master Sommeliers was exposed for a cheating scandal, and in October of 2020, it was exposed again for gross sexual misconduct among multiple male master sommeliers. While sickened and disgusted by the time I spent away from my children and my family to attempt to pass an exam that was set up to fail people rather than to help them succeed, I felt great relief at knowing I had released myself from that organization years ago and had no further involvement.

CHAPTER TWENTY-TWO

Nana

Nana is the original Inez Brown Simmons.

Born in Rexburg, Idaho, she was raised Mormon on a small farm. She attended and graduated from Ricks College (now BYU-Idaho) and joined the Red Cross in 1942. During World War II, she was stationed in North Africa, where she met her husband, Walter Eugene Simmons, a Tarboro native.

The story is that she was running the doughnut and coffee station, and when it was his turn in line, he told her that he would like two doughnuts instead of one.

"You'll get one, Magnolia Mouth, just like everyone else," she told him.

Apparently, that was when the sparks flew and Gene knew Inez was the one.

When the war ended, Gene sent a telegram to his parents saying he was sending home his soon-to-be-wife to live with them until he returned. He also wrote in the telegram that she was Mormon, but they were to make no mention of this when they met her.

Again, the story goes that when my great-grandparents Mr. and Mrs. Simmons picked Inez up from the Rocky Mount train station and she settled into the back seat of their car, the first thing my great-grandfather said to her was, "So you're a Mormon, are you?"

My grandmother responded, "Yes, sir, I am."

"How many wives does your dad have?" he asked.

"My dad only has one wife, but my grandfather had three," Inez said.

"Three?!" my great grandfather exclaimed excitedly, before asking how in the world that worked.

Inez explained that her grandfather lived in a main house on the property, and each wife lived in her own house located close behind the main house. She told my great-grandfather that he employed a runner, and whenever he demanded one of the wives' company, he instructed the runner to go get whichever wife it was.

"Fascinating," my great-grandfather bellowed. "How old did your grandfather live to be?"

"Seventy-seven," Inez said flatly. "But the runner died at eighteen."

My great-grandparents knew then and there that Inez would have no trouble living and making friends in Tarboro and that they would love her like they loved their witty son.

Inez lived in Tarboro for the rest of her life, taking her daughters back to Idaho on the train every summer to visit their cousins and aunts and uncles. I think often about Nana not living with or seeing her family on a regular basis since it's so different from the life I live now, with all my family just a quick drive away. I think how brave she was to build a new life in a new place where she knew no one but her husband, whom she probably didn't know very well either until after marriage.

Being named after her is one of the greatest honors of my life. Our bond grew from the moment I knew how to talk, when I would wake up at 6 a.m. and call her to come pick me up (the first time it happened, my parents didn't know where I was and thought I had been kidnapped) to being at her bed the day before she breathed her last breath.

Nana had big dreams of me becoming the next Katie Couric, but she settled for me opening a well-run dining destination in the town where I was born and raised. Never once did she doubt any career decision I made, including when we opened a brewery two blocks from the restaurant, with her helping to fund it. I spoke to Nana about all of my decisions, and she always financially backed the ones she knew wouldn't get off the ground without her help.

Early on the morning of Saturday, June 29, I was scheduled to fly to New York to attend my dear friend Maggie and Paul's fifth wedding anniversary. It was a special occasion, one I'd been looking forward to ever since I got the invitation.

But when I arrived at Greenville Airport for the first leg of my flight to Charlotte, the woman behind the desk told me there was a scheduling problem, and they were trying to see if they could get a plane to Greenville to fly out at the time of my departure. Confused, I asked them to check Raleigh. I could easily drive to Raleigh and fly from there if there was a direct flight to New York.

For the next two and a half hours, I sat and waited for any news about flights from Greenville or Raleigh to JFK, LaGuardia, or even Newark. Finally, around 11 a.m., the airline attendant told me every flight that day from Raleigh was booked, and no plane would even be coming to Greenville that day.

I had never heard of anything like this, but as I searched airline websites on my phone, I soon found it was true.

I drove back to Tarboro and decided to stop at Nana's briefly before heading home.

When I pulled onto Norfleet Court, I saw my mom at the gate, waiting for me.

"It's time, Inie," she whispered. "It's time for you to tell Nana goodbye."

That Saturday was the last day Nana was coherent. Earlier the night before, her organs had started failing, and hospice had come in to make her comfortable.

I got into the bed with her and told her about the entire New York story.

She looked at me and told me she already knew.

We held hands, and I kissed all over her soft face and wrapped my entire body around her frail one, crying, "Please don't leave me," while she whispered, "There, there."

She was so brave and strong, and I was so weak and broken, and as I write this, I can feel her skin, hear her voice, see her chest rise and fall as she stroked my head.

That afternoon, Stephen called Nana's to tell me a customer had picked up a big catering order and driven it back to their lake house, but the staff had forgotten to load the cupcakes into their car. He asked my mom if I could drive the cupcakes to the customer's lake house an hour away.

Both my mom and my aunt said I needed to go; Nana was tired, and I needed a break from crying.

So, I left her—the last time I would see her as the Nana who could tell me how much she loved me—and drove an hour west, watching the most beautiful sunset of my entire life.

Nana lived to be ninety-four years old. She was so afraid she wouldn't get to enjoy her two great-grandchildren that she willed herself to live to see one grow to almost nine and the other a week from turning six. They both adored her, and my memories of the joy on her face when they were together is one of my greatest blessings.

CHAPTER TWENTY-TWO

Laughter Break! IBS Is Real

Nana died when I was thirty-seven. I loved her with every piece of my body, and when she died, a piece of me died as well. There was a huge void in my world, and because I am who I am, I needed desperately to fill that void. And that is how running came to be a part of my daily routine.

Maybe you have a mental image of what a runner looks like: tall, slender, balanced, and gazelle-like. I might be small-boned, but I am none of those other things. In fact, I am one of the clumsiest individuals on the planet. I trip over both of my feet, and when I fall, it is *not* graceful. I go down in the most awkward and embarrassing fashion. It's a sight to see—but since I've been doing it since I was old enough to walk, I have no shame when it happens.

Another thing about me: When I was twenty-three years old, a young doctor in my small hometown diagnosed me with Irritable Bowel Syndrome, or IBS. I had never heard of it until that appointment, but the diagnosis seemed dead-on. I have the kind of IBS that makes me poop three-plus times a day. Everything I eat goes straight through me. I spend more time going to the bathroom than I do sleeping. I am almost positive I have a gluten intolerance, but I refuse to receive a diagnosis I am adamantly opposed to.

My friends and neighbors Erin and Daniel, meanwhile, are the epitome of my mental image of runners: tall, slender, balanced, gazelle-like, and absolutely beautiful. They're the runners who have been running since college and have trained for and completed marathons. They're what I like to call *professional runners.*

And because they are kind, professional runners, when I expressed my desire to run a marathon before turning forty, they welcomed me into their running rituals.

Erin and Daniel didn't just run, you see—they trained. They had my ass up at four in the morning, jogging to the high school to practice "speed work." What the fuck is speed work, you ask? I honestly don't know, except that every morning after I finished up at the track, I had to sit on the grass next to the sprinkler system with my head between my knees, thinking I was going to pass out.

They had another running term known as "planting water." On the weekends, we would take our "long runs" (another running term, apparently), during which Erin would "plant" water along our route so that we could hydrate at the appropriate checkpoints. Believe you me, I looked forward to our water breaks almost as much as I looked forward to seeing my house at the end of the run.

Some people think running helps you to lose weight. That was not the case for me. When I finished those long runs, I was so hungry I ate triple my regular amount. No, there was no weight loss happening during my marathon training. Instead, I stayed the exact same weight the entire time.

One Saturday evening before a fourteen-mile run, Erin texted to say she would plant water for us. Of course, since we had begun training, Erin had done all of the water planting. I hadn't woken up early to do it once, and I felt the appropriate shame. I texted back saying it was my turn, and I would take care of it.

She must have sensed that there could be complications because she responded that she really didn't mind. No, no, I replied quickly and confidently—*I* would do it.

To this day, I'm not sure why I didn't just let her. That was my first mistake, though it's neither here nor there now. My second mistake? Not having any bottled water in my house to plant.

I got home from the restaurant late that Saturday evening, and before going to bed, I set my alarm for 5:15 a.m. and set out my running clothes and running shoes next to my contact lens case so that everything was in one place and I wouldn't wake Stephen when I arose.

Stephen, by the way, *is not* a runner. He doesn't condone running; he doesn't like to talk about running. And he also has no tolerance for potty humor. In our twelve years of marriage, he has never gone to the bathroom anywhere close to me. My sister once mentioned my IBS in front of him, and he asked if we would never ever bring it up again.

So, I haven't.

What does that have to do with this story?

You'll see.

On Sunday morning, everything went as planned—at first, anyway. I awoke when my alarm went off at 5:15, put in my contact lenses, and dressed in less than ten minutes. Then I jumped into my car and drove to Food Lion to buy bottled water.

CLOSED.

As was the RaceWay Gas Station. As was the Shell Station. As was the Exxon.

YOU HAVE GOT TO BE FUCKING KIDDING ME!

I hadn't even thought about the fact that in a small town like Tarboro, every motherfucking gas station and grocery store is closed before 7 a.m. on Sunday mornings.

Maybe it was this irritation that made the IBS flare up. Maybe it was whatever I ate or drank the night before. Maybe it was just because I lost a bet with God. I don't know, but all of a sudden, I felt it.

I felt the weird, uncomfortable rumbling of a big diarrhea attack.

In true Inie fashion, I tried to dismiss it. I still needed water, for God's sake, and I still needed to plant it.

It was then that I remembered seeing an Aquafina vending machine outside the Food Lion, my original destination.

I left Big Jim's right across the street and sped back over to Food Lion.

At this point, I had started to sweat. I could feel my bowels telling me they were going to win this morning.

What the fuck? The vending machine didn't take ATM cards. It was coins/dollars only, and I didn't have enough muscle control to beat the shit out of the machine and not shit my pants.

I found exactly enough coins to buy one small bottled water and decided then and there that Erin would get it. I deserved to be punished for not being a better planner or planter.

When I drove out of the Food Lion parking lot, I knew it was too late. I was never going to make it. The closest place I could possibly get to in town was my mom and stepfather's house on Main Street—which, for those of you who don't live in towns with a population of ten thousand, is exactly what you would guess: the main street of our community.

During the two-minute drive to my mom's house, sweat was pouring out of my forehead, tears were running down my face, and my asshole was on maximum overdrive working to keep the shit from exploding out of my ass.

As soon as I pulled into her driveway, the poop started its way out of me.

It was 5:36 a.m., and not one light was on in my mom's house.

As soon as I opened the gate to her backyard and got to the nearest tree—where I pulled down my pants and squatted—the shit was everywhere.

It was running down my legs, into my socks, and completely covering my ass, since it had started while I was sitting in the driver's seat of my car.

My mother's two obnoxious dogs were in front of me, barking with a vengeance. This made it possible that not only would my mom and stepdad wake up to find me shitting on a tree in their backyard, but also that their next-door neighbors—who happen to be my best friend's parents—would look out their window to see a thirty-nine-year-old grown-ass woman shitting her brains out on a tree while two dogs barked at her maniacally.

In case you're not sure what total humiliation feels like, this is it.

Once the diarrhea attack ended, I pulled up my poo-soaked shorts and got back into the car to drive home.

No water planted. No self-respect whatsoever.

When I arrived at my house, Erin and Daniel were waiting for me.

My windows were already rolled down, for obvious reasons, and as I pulled up, I asked them to hang out at the curb because I had had a little accident. Of course, they thought I was crazy, but they walked out to the curb to give me a little space.

I opened the door of the car and backed into the house, just in case they were able to see from far away that I had shit my pants.

I went straight to the basement, undressed, threw all my clothes into the washing machine, and started it. I knew very well that if Stephen ever heard about this, he would move out.

Then I tiptoed upstairs, jumped into the shower, and washed off all the poo that had gotten all over me.

Once I had dressed, I knew I had one more thing to do to cover all possible evidence.

I grabbed the 409 and a roll of paper towels and took them out to the car, where I sprayed down the driver's seat and wiped everything clean. I put the dirty paper towels into a plastic bag and threw them away in the outdoor trash receptacle, then I grabbed the lone bottled water and walked it out to the curb to meet Erin and Daniel.

"It's a long story, but I wasn't able to plant any water. I will run carrying the one bottle I have and then give it to y'all to share at the time you deem appropriate."

Honestly, I cannot for the life of me remember what happened next. Did they say we'd just stop at Walgreens and drink from the water fountain?

Possibly.

I don't remember running holding water, but I am honestly not sure.

What I do remember is calling my mother once we got back from our run around 10 o'clock that morning. My stepfather, Bill, answered, and his tone was extremely agitated.

"Where's Mom?" I asked.

"She's at church," he snapped.

"What's wrong with you?"

"The goddamn dogs got into something in the backyard," he shouted, "and vomited all over the goddamn house."

"That's tough," I told him. "Tell Mom to call me when she gets home."

CHAPTER TWENTY-FOUR

My Friend Maggie

Maggie is one of those friends you meet later in life, just when you're starting to think you've made all of your lifelong friends.

I met her at a funeral in September of 2001.

Her longtime boyfriend, Jeff Coale, worked at Windows on the World as an assistant cellar master. He was a beautiful person: sincere, kind, compassionate, and warm. Everyone who worked with him took an instant liking to him. He was also intelligent and gentle, excited about the possibilities that wine had to offer.

Jeffrey was killed on September 11, 2001.

Never wanting to be considered anything but professional, Jeff always came to work early, ready to perform and start the day perfectly so everyone else would benefit from his diligence.

Unfortunately, that meant he came to work early on the morning of September 11.

I remember talking to his girlfriend, Maggie, on the evening of September 11. She was trying to figure out if there was any chance he had been anywhere else besides in the demolished towers.

I don't remember saying anything that could have been comforting. I don't remember saying anything that made any sense.

Two weeks later, Stephen and I drove to a town outside of Philadelphia to celebrate the short life of Jeffrey Coale. I remember walking into the church, where I proceeded to cry until I couldn't cry anymore.

As I wrote earlier, I don't have many regrets in life, but one I do have is not standing up to speak about Jeff at his funeral. You see, most of those who spoke were high school or college friends or family—people who had known Jeff for a long time. I had only known him briefly, but I knew what he was trying to learn as an assistant cellar master. I knew what he had given up in hopes of starting a magical career. I knew that he had thrown caution to the wind to live a dream—a dream that wouldn't make him rich, a dream that would make him tired, but a dream that would bring so much satisfaction—of his ambitions and his senses.

After the funeral, I looked for Maggie, the longtime girlfriend I hadn't met but had heard so much about. As soon as I met her, I felt as if I had known her forever. And I'll never forget the words she spoke to me that day when I said I'd like to meet her parents: "My parents were killed in a plane crash when I was very young, but I would love to introduce you to my aunt and uncle, who raised me after they were killed."

Words cannot describe that feeling. That sickening feeling of learning that not only has someone lost their love, but they had also lost their original loves—the ones who loved them first.

Maggie is special. I knew it then, and I know it now.

She once said something to me that I quote all of the time. "You look to the left, and you find someone who has it better. You look to the right, and you find someone who has it worse."

Right you are, ol' Maggie, but how many people understand that?

Today, Maggie is one of my closest friends, even if I only see her once a year. She's also one of my best reminders that for all the darkness life throws at you, you always have to find laughter. That's partly because Maggie has a mouth on her like no other—and that's saying something, since my mouth never spares cuss words.

Which reminds me of the weekend Maggie, her husband, Paul, and their son, Quintin, came to visit us.

On the Sunday morning, before they went back to New York, we were all hanging out in our living room, with six-year-old Stephen sitting on the ottoman playing a game on the television. Maggie was telling us about one of her rich, glitzy friends who sent their children to a summer camp that cost $20,000. As I tried to catch my breath, sputtering, *"Twenty . . . thousand . . . dollars,"* Maggie announced that she too had been sent to the same summer camp but had gotten kicked out mid-summer.

When I asked why, she loudly proclaimed, "I told the head counselor to go fuck himself."

Had there been a record player in the room, it most certainly would have scratched. Instead, Big Stephen, who worked incredibly hard at sheltering our children from cuss words, immediately started talking loudly about some type of fishing he had once done in order to avoid any commotion around Maggie's comment.

It seemed to have worked, and the conversation continued with very little fanfare. It wasn't until Monday afternoon when I picked the kids up from school that I realized little Stephen had not only heard the entire thing but also ingested it like a Flintstone vitamin.

As Mrs. G.—Mrs. Gianino, a Boston transplant to eastern North Carolina, who taught both our children for pre-K—was buckling Stephen into his car seat, he looked innocently at her and said, "I know a bad word."

I was sure that just like any other teacher, Mrs. G. would look kindly at Stephen and say, "We don't say bad words, my child." Instead, she turned on me like a betrayed friend and said gently, "Tell it to me."

Before my brain could tell my mouth to interrupt, little Stephen looked Mrs. G. squarely in the eye and said, "Gofunkyourself."

"Wow, that is a *bad* word!" Mrs. G. exclaimed as she looked at me with great joy and triumph.

"He learned that from our friend who was visiting from New York this weekend," I blurted out.

"Sure, he did," she said, with absolutely no belief in her voice.

Thanks to text, email, and Facebook, Maggie and I can continue our conversations about life, even though we live so far apart. The night of Osama Bin Laden's death, she wrote to me, "The sky is beautiful and blue, flowers bloom in colors only God could create, and children's giggles warm our hearts."

Maggie is my hero. She overcomes. She prevails. She leads by being an example of forgiveness and strength. When bad things happen, I think about her infinite wisdom. I think about her living life to the fullest, even though she's been hurt so much.

It hurts to imagine a life where I wasn't friends with a girl named Maggie, a girl who always shows me brightness, no matter how dark my world is.

CHAPTER TWENTY-FOUR

Tarboro Brewing Company

I n 2013, not long after Nana died, Stephen and I launched an Indiegogo campaign to help us start a brewery—Tarboro Brewing Company, affectionately known as TBC.

Back in 2008, my father had sold us an old, 10,000-square-foot building a couple of blocks down from On the Square. He had originally bought it because of its incredible charm. At that time, the restaurant was wildly successful, and we were turning away reservations each night we were open. We had many people telling us we had outgrown the space and needed a bigger kitchen and a much bigger dining room.

I think it was a month after we closed on the building that the economy tanked, and no one wanted to invest in a restaurant, period—much less one in poor, rural eastern North Carolina. Plus, Stephen and I were happy owning On

INEZ RIBUSTELLO

the Square with my dad and not having anyone to answer to when it came to labor or food costs.

So, we sat on the building for years, allowing it to be used for community karaoke and private parties that didn't require electricity or a kitchen. While the building was charming, it was also dilapidated.

Over the next couple of years, Stephen and I kept a close eye on the microbrewery explosion happening all over the state of North Carolina, including our eastern part. We started to realize that 526 N. Main Street was the ideal location for a local brewery, as opposed to a fine-dining restaurant.

It just so happened that a peer of mine, Franklin Winslow, who had moved to Pennsylvania to attend boarding school when he was fourteen, still lived in Philadelphia, where he was Director of Quality Assurance for Yards Brewing Company. So, when he came home for Christmas, we approached him to see if he'd come on board our brewery, and he said, "Sure, I'll do it if you can raise the money."

Raising money was fucking hard, especially for someone who had never done it before. We had spent ten years running a local restaurant and wine store that grossed over a million dollars a year, but I had never written a business plan or dealt with outside investors.

So, we started with a crowdfunding campaign, launched in September of 2013, five years after we bought the building from Dad. Thanks to Indiegogo, we raised almost $20,000 in six weeks. This money helped pay for an attorney to draw up the bylaws as well as a shareholder agreement.

From there, we started pitching a fairly modest business plan, mostly to local investors and family. Then, with the help of the Town of Tarboro, we received a $200K grant that was based on job creation, building improvements, and double the investment (i.e., we needed to raise $400K in addition to the $200K grant).

This was a solid puzzle piece that intrigued potential investors, but the problem was Stephen and I had no earthly idea what we were doing, nor did we know how to talk about return on investment. In fact, I was so bad at it, I would go into a meeting and say, "Please don't think about giving us any money if your lifestyle will change because we have no idea if this will work or not."

Stephen put the kibosh on that pitch the first time he heard me say it.

We spent more than a year trying to raise $600,000 to start construction, but right up to the Sunday afternoon we were scheduled to update our investors, we were $225,000 short. I knew, I just *knew*, that we were about to hear the investors say they wanted their money back because the process was taking too long and anyone with sense could see this was a harebrained idea.

Still, the dinner meeting was due to be held at our home, so I went to Food Lion to get supplies for the dinner we were serving. I was in the grocery store parking lot when my cell phone rang. It was a gentleman in Atlanta who had married a woman from Tarboro; I had been a junior bridesmaid in their wedding. I had given her the business plan in May, and she had said she would get in touch soon.

"Soon" just happened to be five months later on the day of the meeting where we were set to tell the investors we were $225,000 short.

"We're in for $100K," he said.

I'm not sure what I said. I'm pretty sure it wasn't coherent.

When I got home, I ran through the backdoor to see Stephen on the phone, waving at me not to talk. I was jumping around like a hyena, trying to let him know I had something urgent to tell him, and he needed to get off the phone immediately.

He ignored me and kept listening to whoever was on the other line.

When he finally hung up, he said, "That was my buddy John. He wants $100,000 worth of shares in TBC."

Two hours before doomsday, we had raised $200,000: one investor in Atlanta and one in New York. Both were long-time friends who believed in us and the project.

As you can imagine, people do a world of talking in our small town, just like any other small town. All of those current investors had heard we were more than $200,000 short, and they were very ready to hear how we were going to start a business without appropriate capitalization. Stephen and I were giddy as we shared the news. Even better: When we announced the $200,000 of investment, it prompted one of our early investors to say she would invest the outstanding $25,000 in her children's names.

And just like that, after years of dreaming and praying, we could finally start creating Tarboro Brewing Company.

That was September of 2014. The next year and a half were tough, marked by the stress of the buildout, the constant fear of running out of money, and the anxiety caused by a few investors second-guessing my every move. Even when we were finally able to start brewing beer in the production facility, our troubles weren't over. Over the course of the three years since we first wrote the business plan, the number of breweries in North Carolina had tripled, and our business model built on wholesale was close to obsolete. Then there was the kicker: We had zero cash left in the bank by the time we were able to start selling beer in February 2016.

I'm not sure if this comes down to the way women are wired, but this felt like the ultimate failure to me. I internalized every single ounce of it, believing that the failure was mine and mine alone. I sent a vulnerable email to investors, explaining the situation and that we desperately needed to open a taproom in the short term. Within a matter of hours, I had raised $125,000. To feel that belief in us and our project was humbling, but for someone who already feels the weight of the world on their shoulders, it also made my load even more heavy.

Now that I look back on it all, I laugh at our naivete and how optimistically foolish we were. But at the same time, I wince. We had no idea of the drain this venture would be on our family—most significantly, our fragile marriage.

CHAPTER TWENTY-SIX

Forty Years Old and in Crisis

arried couples who work together don't often talk publicly about the wear and tear the arrangement can put on a union. Sometimes, they don't even know it themselves. When I look back at 2013, I think about how much heartache we could have prevented had we invested in therapy then and there. But we were young, stubborn, and destined to play out the scripts we inherited.

Opening On the Square, trying to bury 9/11, having children (both unplanned), and studying for the Master Sommelier pin proved to be fairly intense. Then I lost a grandmother who was also my best friend and found myself raising two children who were now able to express their needs, all while working in a high-stress environment where someone was always complaining about something—mostly customers, but sometimes staff too. The soup was already cooking on high heat, and instead of taking a step back and doing some real inner work, we chose the opposite course: We opened a brewery, instantly throwing a gallon of gasoline onto the already burning stove. Even when I gave up the Master Sommelier path, I simply replaced it with opening Tarboro Brewing Company.

Having a homecoming with Jesus during those years gave me more peace than I probably would have had if I were going at life alone, but when I look back at the fifteen years before I turned forty, I can see it was way too much for one person to handle.

Stephen would say the strain on our marriage was directly caused by TBC, but I know that TBC is only a part of it. Had we stayed the course and stuck to just running On the Square, without serious work to make our marriage foundation firm, we would still have burned the soup. It was only a matter of time.

Life hands people enough to deal with, without us creating unnatural additions. I was determined to make sure my life looked the same as it would have if 9/11 hadn't happened—so I created a hectic world full of so much stress, pressure, and longing for more that I didn't have any free time to take care of myself or my marriage.

Stephen didn't seem to mind or care, but once we were able to look back on everything, it became apparent that he too suffered because of my busyness—having a wife who doesn't make time to listen or connect on a regular basis doesn't strengthen a union.

The biggest strain, however, was the constant—and I mean constant—toll of owning a restaurant together where we were both there all the time. The nature of the service industry is that guests feel they have the right to give feedback in any and all situations because they are paying for their food/drink/experience. Whether it was someone calling me while I was watching the kids at awards day saying they needed a booth for their reservation, a neighbor from down the street saying their fish wasn't cooked all the way, or a dear friend asking to buy wine on Christmas Eve after we had closed, our lives were never uninterrupted. A couple of these occurrences happening once a year is one thing, but the nature of running a restaurant in a small town was that these texts, phone calls, and emails were daily events. When Stephen and I were not at On the Square working, we were still working by responding to complaints or needs. It took me years to admit to myself, but this work broke me, and had I not left On the Square in the role I had, it would have completely broken our marriage. So, when it came down to Stephen and me or the restaurant, I chose Stephen and me. And boy, was it a painful choice.

Our unhealthy cycle of life consisted of someone telling me what was wrong with something and then me either going to Stephen with the complaint, which always felt to him like an attack, or me internalizing it on my own, adding an anxiety that stayed with me for days, sometimes weeks.

The cycle was not healthy, not kind, not anything good, but it was a cycle, nonetheless.

By the time all was said and done, our marriage was almost completely over, my love affair with Jesus had come close to death, and my belief in myself had unraveled to the point of vanishing.

It was a devastating time, the loneliest and lowest I had ever experienced because while September 11th was traumatic, at least Stephen and I had and held one another through the pain. Not in this case—Stephen and I separated. The brewery was a newborn, and On the Square was a teenager. That summer, I couldn't have told you my maiden name if you had asked me. I weighed less than 100 pounds, and my only focus was being able to breathe—just like after 9/11. If you asked the children, they would probably say they took care of me during this time, although I'm not sure any of us remember it. We were just living together, loving each other, even though no one understood what the fuck was going on—least of all the children, whose mom had always been a rock until then.

At swim meets, where very few people made an effort to talk to me, Cynthia would pull me over to her chair and sit her lanky twelve-year-old body in my lap, protecting me from stares, glares, and gossip. And little Stephen held my hand everywhere we went, letting me know he wouldn't let anyone hurt my feelings on his watch. But when they weren't around, I felt the isolation, through the disappointed looks and the shaking of heads when I passed people on Main Street.

Because of personal choices that are too sensitive to share with others outside of my immediate circle, I choose not to write words that could and would inflict hurt or pain.

But I will say these choices also complicated the health of the brewery, and I caught hell and then some from a few investors who felt the need to assert their male dominance.

The strongest man throughout that hellacious summer of 2016 just happened to be Stephen, who was experiencing such deep pain and loss, but through it all, he never wavered.

We found a truly exceptional therapist, who we had reached out to, to help us co-parent, and because of forgiveness, a desperation for holding on, and our therapist's intense work, we were able to come out of the fire alive with a few minor burns and ultimately, a much better marriage.

Without my children, who for whatever reason felt very protective of me, I'm not sure I would have stayed in Tarboro. The easiest thing to do would have been to run away, but my feet wouldn't do it, most likely because my heart told them the painful story of a mother who had run away years ago when the world had failed her.

And so, I slept. I slept more than I had slept in the past twenty years. It was as if my brain had said to my body, "Either we sleep, or we leave . . . you choose." And the sleep came more easily than it ever had. It came without guilt or shame or heartache. In fact, it replaced all of those feelings. Those feelings were all I felt when I was awake.

But as well as the hardest time of my life, that summer was also my greatest evolution into my real self. I found out who my real friends were, and I developed a self-confidence I never imagined I could have. I also found my voice, a voice I had hushed so often just to keep the peace. That summer helped me understand it was more important to speak up and speak out than to keep silent.

And, of course, I also found Glennon. In the work of Glennon Doyle, author of *Carry On, Warrior* and *Love Warrior*—which was released during my personal hell—I found the solace of knowing that I could break into a million pieces, and I could also rebuild.

And I had a lot to rebuild. I started going to my own personal therapy to deal with my crumbling marriage, but I ended up doing the most intense work of my life, going back to age four. The irony was that in the end, 9/11 was the least of it.

The truth will set you free.

But first, it will take you into the depths of hell.

I was forty years old when I stopped running away, stopped searching desperately for anything that would take me back up north. Maybe it was a midlife crisis. All I know is that all of a sudden, I didn't know who I was or even how I got to be in my body.

Once I confided in someone, I was able to breathe again.

Was this what wisdom really meant?

The ability to speak the truth aloud?

The ability to ask for help?

Stephen's and my ship was built in 2001—and yet in the same year, it was determined to sink.

The other details are too sensitive for others outside of my direct circle, so, again, I choose not to share them.

But that time is part of my story, and I want to let others know I was able to survive the depths of hell in a marriage and come out of it not just alive but with a healthier union between my husband and me.

It wasn't easy, and it required both of us to dig into our painful childhoods, to go back deep to find our triggers and our stories.

Stephen and I both had thought 9/11 was the big rupture that we had found a way to survive, but in our thirteenth year of marriage, we discovered that we had buried so many of the wounds of our childhoods, we were guaranteed to reenact our parents' scripts.

As you can imagine, my children, my parents, my husband, and my friends all struggled immensely with my becoming unraveled because I had been an anchor for so long. It was terrifying for them to watch me become unreliable and unpredictable.

But that's the thing I now understand that I didn't for a long time (thank you, Glennon Doyle): I wasn't meant to live the life I was living, where I worked only to please, never to be pleased. I had become exhausted with the life I had created for myself. It was just not working for me. And these feelings of despair, self-loathing, fear, suffocation, and angst crippled my brain, handicapped my heart, and ultimately saved me from my own destruction.

The aftermath was ugly.

Relationships changed, or relationships ended.

But what I know now is that the relationships that mattered not just survived but morphed into the healthiest relationships I have ever had.

It wasn't easy; in fact, it was brutal, but when I reflect back on the summer of '16, I wouldn't trade that deep loneliness for anything. Because that loneliness, as brutal as it was, saved me.

It saved my marriage.

It saved my family.

And most importantly, it saved my almost-broken spirit.

And that, my friends, is when life got real.

Not real in the fact that it got hard or fast or exciting.

Real in the sense that I started living my life, building my businesses, and choosing my people in a way I believed in. Authentically. Genuinely. Intentionally.

And that is when the rest of my life began.

And part of the rest of my life was TBC: embarking on my mission to make, yes, a kickass brewery—but more than that, a safe community space where race relations in our small town could start the healing process.

CHAPTER TWENTY-SEVEN

Mulligans and Heaven Blog Post

When Stephen and I first met, we were working together at Windows on the World, and we shared an office on the 106th floor of One World Trade Center. When we met in June of 2000, about the only thing we had in common was our love of fermented grape juice.

I was from eastern North Carolina and thought Chicken Tetrazzini was the best thing I had ever eaten; he was from the Hudson Valley region of New York, where he grew up on liver and stuffed shells.

If you had asked me what a stuffed shell was, I would have said a hermit crab.

Stephen moved at a faster pace than I did, whereas I was the nerdy type, afraid of getting into trouble or doing the wrong thing.

If any of you had seen us during the first few months together, you would have said we had about as much chance of being a couple as Shiraz and Viognier. We were completely different people from two completely different worlds, and our only likeness was our love of wine.

So, I guess that's where you can say wine is pretty magical.

As the days turned into months, I found Stephen to be extremely funny. He was quirky, yes, but he also had a hilarious sense of humor, constantly shocking my lips into curved smiles.

It took a while, but after six months, I could not deny the fact that I absolutely loved this sommelier, who knew more about wine than anyone I had ever met.

We took the plunge, and after convincing ourselves we could go out without anyone else's knowledge, we decided to become exclusive.

I will never forget our conversation after almost a year of dating.

We had gone out one night, and I had acted like a complete fool . . . super mean and completely obnoxious.

As per usual, one wakes up the next day, realizing they didn't make a great showing the night before.

I apologized profusely, and I asked him if he was going to be able to forgive me and continue to be my boyfriend.

His answer is one I will always remember.

He asked, "Do you know what a mulligan is?"

"Is it a bird?" I wondered aloud.

"Close," he said. "It is when you swing your club in golf and it is such a bad shot that you don't have to count it. You can take another one with no penalty."

"You," he said to me, "have a never-ending amount of mulligans."

And that was the day, the day I knew I would marry this man who would forgive me of all my faults and flaws.

Rewind to thirty-five years ago, long before I met Stephen.

The setting is the dining room in Tarboro, circa 1980.

My grandparents, affectionately known as Gran and Papa Bear, are the players and they are eating supper with friends and family.

Gran asked Papa Bear, "Do you think you will know me in heaven?"

Papa Bear beamed at her and said, "It won't be heaven if I don't."

Love comes in many sayings and with many words. I will always appreciate hearing any that have to do with the unconditional and the other-worldly.

Stephen never met my grandfather, but I think he would love to know he tied him with one of the most romantic sayings my ears have ever heard.

CHAPTER TWENTY-EIGHT

Laughter Break! Headlice, Bagel's Genitalia, and Periods

Because the universe is extremely witty—and because in my life, tragedy has always come hand in hand with comedy—I also had the misfortune of getting a raging case of head lice during this time of extreme social isolation.

In case you're wondering who your true friends are, if there's someone who is willing to do a lice treatment on your head at any time in your friendship, count your blessings. Yes, that's right: At some point during the terrible summer of 2016, my dear friend Jennifer had to take me up to her bedroom and spend hours combing nits out of my hair. If that wasn't demoralizing enough, her husband Jeff walked in the bedroom while she was spraying lice detangler only to make a horrified expression and then walk out.

And if you think that was the first and last time the universe played a joke on me, think again. Family life has been full of laughs—some of them not so comfortable.

In May of 2014, our new permanent minister, Ben, his wife, Lydia, and their daughter, Margot, moved to Tarboro from Nashville, Tennessee. A young couple in their thirties, both Ben and Lydia attended divinity school. As well as joining my church, they also bought a house on our street, South Howard Circle, which they shortly nicknamed SoHo. When they moved in, Margot was two and a half—one of those really smart two-and-a-half-year-olds. The ones who clearly know more than the adults in the room.

Stephen and I invited their family of three to our house for dinner one late spring evening and were delighted when they accepted. By this point, we were happy dog owners. Earlier that year, we had picked up a Dachshund from a farm outside of Rocky Mount because the children (and I) were dying for a pet dog. I brought him home on a cold winter day in February, and the kids squealed and squealed, and within hours of his homecoming they had decided to name him Bagel.

While the owner of the dog assured me that Bagel was a hundred percent Dachshund, it became evident once he grew bigger that there was definitely some Beagle in his genes— slash genitalia. And even though the vet advised us to neuter Bagel, I held on to the possibility of one day finding a nice girl Dachshund so that Bagel could give us the granddogs I so wanted.

But I digress. The point is: Bagel is not neutered.

When two-and-a-half-year-old Margot came to our house for the first time, she was immediately drawn to Bagel, loving his short height and his long body, not to mention his incredible beauty and loving personality. Margot followed Bagel around the living room while Stephen and I sat in the adjacent kitchen with Ben and Lydia, getting to know them better.

At some point during our conversation, I heard Margot asking little Stephen (who was an immature seven-year-old) what were the round things swinging between Bagel's back legs.

Before I could interrupt, little Stephen replied, in a voice reminiscent of *Beavis and Butt-Head,* "Heh heh heh, go ask your dad."

Thinking I had just survived a near miss, I watched as Margot walked over to Ben and asked, "Dad, what are those two round things swinging between Bagel's back legs?"

Little Stephen's ears perked up in great anticipation of Ben's answer, and when Ben replied, "Margot, those are called testicles," little Stephen's face contorted in confusion. "*Mom,*" he yelled at me, "*you told me* it was called a ball sack!"

Jesus, take the wheel.

Fortunately, neither Ben nor Lydia judged us, and fortunately for little Stephen, he heard the correct terminology that night.

Several years later, Ben and Lydia got a second round from little Stephen.

Stephen and I were outside putting up the new slackline he had received as a Christmas present from his Aunt Kate and Uncle Tommy. Ben and Lydia walked down to our house, now with two little girls (their daughter Phoebe was born in June 2015) who wanted to jump on our trampoline.

We were all standing around talking—Margot, Phoebe, Little Stephen, Ben, Lydia, and me—when Ben asked where Cynthia was. Without missing a beat, he said, "She's in her room masturbating."

Well, there you go, folks. Just in case you think it couldn't get any more awkward in front of your minister and his wife, I present to you this incredible scenario.

Then there was the time little Stephen figured out what it meant when a girl was having her period.

Every year on the day after Christmas, my family loves to drive to a neighboring town and watch a matinee. It's my sister's Christmas gift to her nieces and nephews, since she loves watching movies as much as my dad loves eating Vienna sausages for breakfast.

That year, she wanted to take the children to see the musical *The Greatest Showman*. I despise movies like that. I really, really do. So, I told her that I would be going to *Pitch Perfect 3* instead.

Little Stephen, who was ten at the time, opted to go with me. My son and I have always shared a love for popular television shows and movies.

Was this the appropriate movie to take a ten-year-old boy to see? Well, personally, I think "appropriate" is a highly misused word.

And so, in a very crowded movie theater, snuggled together with our popcorn, Junior Mints, and shared Coca-Cola, we settled in for what we knew would be a solid hour and forty-five minutes of laughter.

For those of you who haven't seen it, in the opening scene, a female character is trying to explain to her rapper client why his song is a steaming pile of shit when her boss jumps in to tell him that she's on her period.

"Mom, what's a period?" Stephen whispered loudly enough so that everyone in the rows behind and in front of us could hear.

I never leave a question unanswered, so I very quietly whispered back, "It's something that happens to females once a month that affects their moods and can make them disagreeable."

"Ohhhhhhhh, Cynthia must have that," he loudly exclaimed, as if he'd just made the discovery of a lifetime about his thirteen-year-old sister.

Sometime after that, Cynthia was at the breakfast table one morning eating her bowl of Lucky Charms, the cereal of choice at our house.

I had poured a bowl for Stephen but was waiting for him to come to the table before I poured milk on it.

Eventually, he arrived, unperturbed by the school day ahead of him.

I poured the milk on his cereal and he proceeded to eat it with his hand, shaping his palm like a spoon to hold the liquid in the bowl.

This sight sent Cynthia into a fit of rage—quite something to behold, if you ask me.

Her little face turned bright red, and she yelled, "It's called a spoon—use one!"

To which Little Stephen calmly looked up and retorted, "It's called a period—you're on yours!"

Thank you, *Pitch Perfect 3*. Thank you very, very much.

CHAPTER TWENTY-NINE

My Friend Veronica

When I was twelve years old, I found out a girl in my class was pregnant.

Her name was Veronica, and she was easily the smartest person in our grade. She was tall, fierce, bold, bright, brave, and, now, pregnant. My mind began performing somersaults, trying to understand how this could happen to someone who had such an incredible future ahead of her.

I was small, flat-chested, insecure, and at least a year and a half away from getting my period—something I thought would bring me confidence if I could just go ahead and get it.

I found out in the fall that she was pregnant, and sometime in early March, Veronica stopped coming to school. We asked our sixty-year-old teacher, Mrs. Moore, if Veronica was having her baby now, and she told us it was none of our business.

But we disagreed. We had spent the past six months asking Veronica if we could touch her stomach and feel the baby move. She always let us, and we would marvel that someone our age had a person growing inside them.

Dustin Rashad Higgs was born on March 14, 1989, and named after Dustin Hoffman and Phylicia Rashad. Veronica said she wanted Dustin to be an actor when he grew up, and she was trying to seal his fate by naming him after two great actors.

For the next five years, we would ask Veronica about Dustin and what new tricks he was learning. When we were seniors in high school, she took Dustin to kindergarten. During this entire time, Veronica made straight As, made all-conference in volleyball and basketball, participated in student government, and scored a 1400 on the SAT. With the exception of giving birth and a few weeks following, I'm not sure she missed another day of school. When I think of unicorns or Wonder Woman or heroines in fairy tales, my mind goes straight to Veronica.

Veronica's dream was to attend UNC-Chapel Hill, and our senior year, she was one of three people in our class nominated for the prestigious Morehead-Cain Scholarship. It was 1994, and while affirmative action was all the rage, I assure you there were still plenty of systems in place to knock down a young black woman in rural eastern North Carolina. Veronica was eliminated in the first round because there was a clause in the scholarship saying recipients couldn't have been married, and apparently, having a child made Veronica close enough to having been married to disqualify her from receiving a full ride to the college of her dreams.

Fortunately, Veronica received enough scholarship money to attend anyway, and in August of 1994, she and I would both enroll at the University of North Carolina at Chapel Hill.

We slipped into very different orbits once we got there. I lived in a private dormitory called Granville Towers, joined a sorority, spent most of my nights drinking at bars using a fake ID, and arrogantly decided which classes I would attend on any given day. Veronica, meanwhile, lived in Hinton James (the dorm most freshmen believed to be the worst on campus since it was close to the football stadium with few amenities), volunteered as a manager on the women's basketball team, studied at all hours of the night at Davis Library, and never missed a class or an opportunity to meet with her TAs.

We would get together for lunch at Sutton's Pharmacy once a semester to drink vanilla Cokes and eat cheeseburgers while catching up on one another's lives. Her mom and dad were taking care of Dustin while Veronica lived on campus, working to be the first-generation college graduate in her family. She bore such a weight of emotion and responsibility on her shoulders, needing to succeed not just for her parents, grandparents, and siblings, but for her son as well.

My senior year in college, I attended the Phi Beta Kappa ceremony to support my boyfriend, who was receiving this esteemed honor. It didn't surprise me one bit when they called Veronica's name to walk across the stage. I screamed, cheered, clapped, whooped, and beamed with joy watching my childhood friend receive the same honor as my wealthy, white, private-school-graduate boyfriend. If only the audience knew Veronica's story, I felt they would be as excited as I was.

Veronica's story is not mine to tell—it's Veronica's, her heroic journey. Whenever she shares it, she does so without any self-pity, resentment, or desire for sympathy, sharing it simply and matter-of-factly. And while I respect and admire that, I also want the privileged people who hear it to understand—really understand—that she overcame incredible obstacles and roadblocks that they never even encountered, thanks to the many variables people who look like me have a hard time recognizing and admitting.

Both of us graduated in spring of 1998, but Veronica stayed in Chapel Hill to attend law school whereas I moved to Manhattan to attend culinary school. By the time she had graduated and passed the bar, I had become a certified sommelier and was running the beverage department at Windows on the World. The next step in Veronica's career was to move to Atlanta, Georgia, to become an attorney with General Motors.

In October of 2004, our ten-year high school reunion was held in Tarboro, and the Friday night after-party was held at On the Square. Veronica and I hadn't seen one another or spoken since the spring afternoon in 1998 when she became Phi Beta Kappa.

By 2004, I was twenty-eight years old and a brand-new mother of a one-month-old. I couldn't wait to see Veronica—I desperately needed to ask her how she had navigated life with a baby. Here I was, twenty-eight years old, married, living in the same town as my parents, and yet, still, I felt so suffocated and scared having another human relying on me to keep them alive. In typical, graceful Veronica style, she smiled at me compassionately and gave all the glory to God and her mom as her only compasses.

Since then, Veronica and I have stayed in touch, and we meet up whenever she comes back to Tarboro. In 2017, she ran for district court judge of Gwinnett County. For six months, she was the only woman in the lineup of candidates before a wealthy white woman with deep Georgian roots entered the campaign in March—almost undeniably an attempt to block Veronica's trajectory to becoming the clear winner.

In May, the election resulted in a runoff between Veronica and this woman.

Our longtime friend Tamika and I drove to Gwinnett County in July to campaign on the day of the runoff.

That evening, we watched Veronica give a concession speech. I sobbed furious tears, not just over the election but also over her elimination from the Morehead-Cain Scholarship and all the unfair disadvantages she had faced before and after.

Tamika and I drove back to North Carolina the following day, both of us acknowledging the fucked-up privilege of the wealthy white woman beating the hard-working black woman who had never been given anything and had been in the race for its entirety, meaning her campaign spending far outweighed her opponent's. Tamika never showed any resentment toward me during that nine-hour drive. I'm not sure I would have been as graceful had the roles been reversed.

In 2020, Veronica ran for Gwinnett County state court judge and won.

But just before she won, George Floyd was murdered.

I remember not knowing what to say to her after the world broke again. By this time, Veronica had two younger sons in addition to Dustin—RJ was thirteen and Dawson was nine. It was at least a week before I mustered up the courage to text her, and when I asked about the boys, she responded saying how terribly frightened they were.

While 2020 didn't disappoint on the sadness meter, my transformation came in the way of anger and activism. For the first time in my adult life, I threw popularity to the wind and chose to speak out against systemic racism via my social media feeds. I'm not sure I could have looked Veronica in the eye again if I didn't. The saddest part of it was that it took me forty-four years to learn that, in my whole life, my silence had been inaction and betrayal to my friends of color.

CHAPTER THIRTY

Pandemic

On March 25, 2020, I released a statement on Instagram Live:

Dear people feeling scared, alone, helpless, and angry,

It's me, Inez—someone who has felt these feelings with great intensity and great longevity. I'm a small business owner in Tarboro, North Carolina. I'm the founder and president of Tarboro Brewing Company, and my husband, Stephen, and I purchased our restaurant, On the Square, seventeen years ago. We employ many amazing people in our town of eleven thousand.

The place we find ourselves in right now, today, feels eerily similar to a place I've been in the past. Restaurants are my world, and my restaurant world collapsed on September 11, 2001, when the greatest job I had ever known fell into the depths of hell along with the building that housed it.

My world literally crumbled as I watched on the television, and I couldn't form a single thought, much less a sentence, on what I could do to make it better.

Seventy-three of my coworkers lost their lives that day, on a workforce more than five times that size.

By no means am I comparing 9/11 to the humanity-scaled crisis of COVID-19. But although the situation surrounding 9/11 is vastly different from the circumstances of our current global pandemic, the feelings I had in 2001 are bubbling back to the surface now. So many of us are feeling helpless, uncertain, unstable. The situations are different, but many of the feelings are the same.

Jobs lost, work families broken up with a great chance of never being reunited, morale in the gutter . . . Life as we know it has changed in ways we never imagined. This was also very much my reality nineteen years ago when the World Trade Center fell.

I have sought out my journals from that time to see what advice I can give now—how I might assuage the fear, the loneliness, the depression. But the only comforting words I can find are the ones given to me by so many of you in 2001 when you wrote and called to say, "You are not alone, and you will survive."

I remember looking at the people who said this to me, thinking they had no idea what they were saying. To be honest, I didn't believe them at all.

But they continued to say it.

And I continued to get out of bed each morning.

And I continued to go to bed each night.

And I continued to breathe.

And at some point, I started feeling whole again.

Not immediately, but gradually.

My friends, we cannot control what's happening all over our world right now.

All we can control is our reaction to it.

And that will most certainly control the outcome.

(All credit for this wisdom goes to my favorite high school football coach.)

Yes, the landscape is going to be very different on the other side.

It's going to look empty and desolate and dark.

But it won't stay that way.

It can't stay that way if we continue to breathe and lift one another up. To encourage our neighbors in all the ways we know are possible.

The reach and impact of this video surprised me as much as it did anyone else. Though I rarely see or speak to my Windows community now, they reached out en masse to tell me that my words touched exactly how they were feeling. Because I am who I am, I was really energized to know I had helped people feel the emotions that were bubbling up from their hearts. If there's anything I've excelled at since 9/11, it's being a rock in the midst of tragedy.

Angel Santiago, one of the head bartenders at the Greatest Bar on Earth—a beautiful man who while never rude was most certainly aloof—messaged me out of nowhere to say:

*Hello Inez, I wanted to reach out to you. Your
video brought me so many different feelings and
emotions. I can't even begin to tell you. Yesterday
I broke into a deep anxiety that I haven't felt
since 9/11. In the grocery store, I broke down.
Couldn't contain myself. Thank you for your
words. They brought me comfort and spirit. We
will overcome and rebound.*

I hadn't seen Angel since September 5, 2001, the day I
flew out of NYC back home to Tarboro for my sister's wedding. Now, we exchange messages often, checking in on how
we're faring and feeling.

This is how I believe the universe works: If you put out
good energy, you receive good energy in the form of friendship in return.

The pandemic also impacted my work.

Fortunately, I'm not motivated by money.

Unfortunately, I *am* motivated by a fear of disappointing
others.

Since the brewery opened in 2016, hemorrhaging cash, I
had lost sleep, lost weight, lost confidence, and lost my hope
of building a successful brewery. Strangely enough, the pandemic and "shelter in place" orders actually took care of a lot
of that for me.

I had already been working with a leadership coach who
had helped me find my way back to feeling confident about
leading the brewery to be a profitable business. The pandemic

brought something different: a sense of acceptance, perhaps, or maybe even comfort. Businesses were closing left and right, even at the onset. It made me feel that if TBC closed now, I had an easy out—a legitimate excuse to explain to people why the business didn't make it.

This is all to say that while COVID-19 took a toll on me in some ways, I didn't end up spiraling into a heap, wondering how the country would survive it. Our country survived 9/11, for Pete's sake. We were most certainly going to survive a pandemic.

And when it comes to my family, the four of us responded to the pandemic in four very different ways:

Stephen rose to the occasion and started working at On the Square 24/7, embracing take-out and home deliveries of provisions. And the wine shop had never had as busy a March as March 2020.

I furloughed myself and started working on Paycheck Protection Program applications for three businesses: On the Square, Tarboro Brewing Company in Tarboro, and TBC West in Rocky Mount. I still rode my bike to the brewery daily to check in, but I did the majority of my work from home, on the computer and the phone, mostly with our two bankers, trying to figure out how and if we were going to get the fucking money to stay afloat for two more months.

It didn't help that Cynthia and I had been in New York visiting Columbia and working the La Paulée Burgundy festival the week before shelter in place was implemented and we returned sick as dogs. Both of us felt terrible and had no idea what was ailing us.

Cynthia continued her studies online, not missing a beat. As well as keeping up with school, she finished her application to the North Carolina School of Science and Mathematics and worked at On the Square, running the register for takeout service at night.

Little Stephen dropped out of school the moment online education went live and logged so many hours on *Fortnite* in the first month of lockdown that the PlayStation died in April, with no chance of resuscitation. I may someday, by request, release video evidence of me losing my shit with him three weeks into March—but I'll have to block my parents from seeing it as it's one of the many times I have dropped the F-bomb on little Stephen in a fit of rage. The scenario goes as follows:

Though I wasn't a nervous wreck about money and the business operations, I did feel like total death, and when I am sick, I am not a nice or patient person. I had been as short and as impatient as any working mother with two kids at home could possibly be, and one morning, I went into Stephen's room to tell him I would like to make it up to him by doing something nice.

His request: a trip to the Speedway to buy a Dunkin' Donuts Boston Creme.

Easy enough—except when we arrived, the Dunkin' Donuts display case sat empty. This was yet another direct result of COVID-19: There would be no display of donuts for dirty kids (and adults, mind you) to reach in and touch—with or without deli paper—and breathe all over before picking one to place on the counter at the gas station register.

Oh, COVID-19, how could you?

With no donuts to make reparations, and knowing I had to be on a conference call with other businesses about PPP applications in fifteen minutes, I made a deal with the devil and told Stephen I would drive him to Rocky Mount (twenty minutes away) to get Krispy Kreme *if* he would "be good" while I was on the conference call.

He agreed.

First stop, however, was DrugCo to pick up prescription medicine to help me feel at least somewhat sane.

At the DrugCo drive-through, I asked the woman if she could sell me any hand sanitizer and tissue. She explained to me that by law, she could only sell one of each per customer, and I said I understood and would take whatever she was able to sell me, along with a bottled water. We pulled out of the drive-through and I popped a few pills, opened the Kleenex box to get a tissue, and doused my hands with hand sanitizer before starting the drive to Rocky Mount. Stephen sat alongside me in the front seat, seemingly happy to be out of the house and in the car headed to Krispy Kreme, where we would most definitely order a dozen donuts.

I dialed in the number to the conference call, put the phone on speaker, and hit the mute button as we cruised down Highway 64 at a comfortable 79 miles per hour.

At one point, I looked over at Stephen, who had doused one of the tissues in hand sanitizer and had it in his mouth, sucking on it like a caramel apple lollipop.

"Really, Stephen? Really? Get that out of your mouth right now. You already know we don't do that."

He already knew we didn't do that because his fourth-grade teacher had called me years ago to tell me that Stephen was sucking on hand sanitizer at school and could I please get him to stop. Not one of my finer moments as a parent, but who's judging?

He grinned at me and took the Kleenex out of his mouth.

I went back to driving and listening until, three minutes later, I smelled something odd.

Did I mention we were going 79 miles per hour down a highway?

I looked over at Stephen, who had found a pilot lighter on the floor (please don't ask, I have no answers) and lit the Kleenex soaked with Purell, which was now legitimately on fire (i.e., throwing out huge-ass flames) in the front seat.

"Losing it" isn't an adequate expression for the way my head almost came off my neck as I screamed in a voice neither of us recognized, "ROLL DOWN THE FUCKING WINDOW! ROLL DOWN THE MOTHERFUCKING WINDOW!"

In Stephen's defense, he actually moved quickly, and within milliseconds, he had the window down and the fire starter thrown out—but not before burning a massive hole in the center of his shorts, directly over his crotch.

Had law enforcement been near us at the time, I'm not sure who they would have arrested, little Stephen or me. Thankfully, no troopers were on the highway that morning.

I looked at Stephen, who was trying to hide his grin from me.

Then I looked back at my phone. Fortunately, it was still on mute.

When I tell my girlfriends this story, the number one question is, "Well, did you get the donuts?"

My answer is always the same: "What kind of mother do you think I am? Donuts are never not gotten."

CHAPTER THIRTY-ONE

Black Lives Matter

This chapter is dedicated to Louise Belcher, Queenie, Hattie, Mary, Lena, and Johnson, the black women and man who sacrificed time away from their families to help raise me.

Some people will hate this book simply because of this chapter.

My only offering to you is that I encourage you to read this chapter anyway. Maybe, just maybe, a seed will be planted.

The night after George Floyd was murdered, I sat on the couch in my living room, my face stinging with tears, half-drunk on Cava, and I reposted a tweet from Bernice King. The tweet featured two photographs: one showing the officer with his knee on Mr. Floyd's neck, and beside it, a picture of Colin Kaepernick kneeling in his football uniform. The tweet read, "If you're unbothered or mildly bothered by the first knee, but outraged by the second, then, in my father's words, you're 'more devoted to order than to justice.' And more passionate about an anthem that supposedly symbolizes freedom than you are about a Black man's freedom to live."

The anger I felt and still feel raged over me as I reposted, typing my own words underneath: "Tired of being scared to post about what I believe to be true. Sick of witnessing injustice, inequity, and full-out white privilege. Sick. And. Tired. If you're not angry, you're just not paying attention."

That was the moment things shifted for me personally, and then for our businesses. It was in this moment that I found a small voice that had been so silent. And as soon as I started to use it, that small voice almost deafened me with shame and guilt that I had taken forty-four years to find it.

On the afternoon of Sunday, June 7, our small town held an Empathy March to pay tribute to George Floyd and the countless other Black Americans before him who have been murdered. That afternoon, when we wrote *Black Lives Matter* on our windows at Tarboro Brewing Company, I felt two truths deep in my soul: First, that these words were there to let my Black brothers and sisters know that we stand with them and that while we cannot possibly feel the pain they're feeling, we see it, we recognize it. Second, that Black Lives Matter has never been a political issue to me. It is simply a matter of humanity.

The uproar that ensued among my white community made it crystal clear that this was not the case for many of them.

I've committed many, many sins in my forty-four years of living. I have done some really fucked-up, shitty-ass things in my life—things that have caused great pain and even destroyed some of my closest relationships. And yet nothing, absolutely nothing, has made my white neighbors as angry as writing *Black Lives Matter* on our taproom windows.

There was a real-life boycott of our business. Then there were the anonymous letters, social media bashing, looking the other way at the grocery store, parents telling their children they couldn't play with little Stephen. I heard, read, and saw the white community saying things like, "I can't play music at your brewery because of the sign," and, "I'm not buying anymore beer because of your sign." Hell, one of our investors tried to give away his $50,000 investment because of the sign.

At my son's global school, a group of white parents actively tried to get our principal fired because she wore a Black Lives Matter mask on the first day of school after the summer break in 2020. This caused such an uproar among these white parents that for almost the entire school year, they called school board members and Central Office saying she jogged during school hours and didn't require enough instruction time for virtual students—all because she publicly stated that Black lives matter. These people were willing to make up lies and jeopardize a woman's job because she supported her Black students, parents, and teachers. One white mom even shared with the school board that she feared her white child didn't feel as valued as his Black peers.

These are the same parents who would not come to the brewery.

What world had I been living in? How did I not know how very real racism is in America and in the small town I have loved longer than any other place in the world? I had been embarrassingly oblivious to the hate people have endured because of their brownness, and the anger I felt over George Floyd, Breonna Taylor, and Ahmaud Arbery turned into disgusted shame over my privilege, entitlement, and full-on ignorance—by which I mean the fact that I ignored a red-hot problem that was right in front of me my entire life.

And then there's the bigger shame, the painful truth I'm still trying to own and combat in myself: Had I known what would happen when we put BLM on the windows, I'm not sure I would have done it.

But it wasn't just angry white people who responded to my social media posts and the message on our windows. My childhood friend Tamika was the first brown friend to text me. It was Tuesday, May 26, at 8:18 p.m.

> *Hi love . . . just checking on you. You crossed my mind.*

My Black friend was checking on me. What the fucking *fuck*? I responded:

Hi, my beautiful friend. I love you. Going to bed, but grateful for friends like you. Love you the most. Heavy, heavy, heavy heart. To be honest, I'm just too embarrassed to talk to my friends of color. I'm so sorry, Tamika. I'm so sorry and ashamed.

And then this:

You have nothing to be ashamed of. You can only do and speak for you. Mom and I just had this conversation. White privilege is a THING and is something the world finds hard to acknowledge. I told her I know that not all white ppl are bad and/or racist . . . but incidents like this make it very difficult to NOT think that. I love you, and I know you are a good person, and you love and do for all. Just wish there were more like you. I appreciate you more than you will ever know, and I would go to the grave for you. There are some real shitty white ppl out there, but I thank God I know some good ones. It's really sad and tiring to wake up and to walk outside not knowing whether you will make it back home safely because of the color of your skin. I think about that every day . . . and I'm a female. Our black males are targets more than us, and it's pathetic! Don't you dare feel afraid to speak your mind. Anybody that turns on you

*for standing for what's right doesn't deserve your
presence in the first place.*

"I wish there was a vaccine for racism," texted my dear friend Bev when she saw *Black Lives Matter* painted on the brewery's windows. "Thank you," she texted, "for posting that on your business windows."

And other members of the Black community found many ways to tell us what our courage meant to them.

Courage? I thought. *This isn't courage. This is too little, too late.*

When my dear friend Tamika texted me in June saying she wanted to tell me how proud she was of my sister Burton and me for being vocal on social media, I asked her if she hadn't known all along that we felt this way. Her response stopped me in my tracks:

"Yes, Inie, your Black friends know your heart, but they didn't know if you'd tell your white friends."

At one point, little Stephen asked my dad why all the racism and injustice toward Black people didn't get worked out completely in the sixties. My dad's answer broke my heart.

"White people got tired," he told my thirteen-year-old son. "They got tired of doing the right thing."

My fear as I write this in May 2021 is that white people are getting tired again. We've seen it happen before. And I'm as guilty as anyone: My Instagram feed has gone back to pictures of my wedding day and my daughter leaving for school, and my Stories are more about promoting my businesses than social justice. I feel myself wondering, is my BLM mask creating more division than heart change?

I feel shame and guilt, and yet I go about my life anyway, knowing good and well that Black folks are more exhausted than anyone. That they have been fighting for their lives from the moment they were born into this world.

I've heard people say that everyone should have to either work in the service industry or serve in the military to become a fully rounded human. After a lifetime in the service industry, I'm going to go a step further and say that everyone should have to spend time in a multicultural community—a community where they are not part of the dominant race. Maybe then, we would all get closer to understanding the constant struggle our brown and Black brothers and sisters face.

The doubting Christian in me has had many dark thoughts during this season of despair. The darkest is that if Jesus himself came down and yelled from the steps of the Capitol that Black lives matter, these people would decide to denounce Jesus too. This is the darkest thought because it makes me believe that there's no hope for us, the white race, to truly love as the universe desires us to love.

I have also returned to two scriptures during this time. The first is the story of Noah and his ark. It's another dark thought, but a real and recurring one for me: Will it take God wiping out the planet and starting over again for people to realize that denying opportunities and even life to people of color is as unchristian as denouncing Jesus?

The other is the story of Saul becoming Paul. This thought is a little more encouraging: Could God decide to blind these people until they eventually see the light—that Black lives have always and will always matter?

CHAPTER THIRTY-TWO

Change (Blog Post, 6/25/2011)

s I write this, my daughter comes to lie in my lap, awakened by a loud clap of thunder signaling the rain that for weeks I've been thirsting for.

She looks at our dog, Simba, as if he's a hero and welcomes him into the living room.

I, on the other hand, cringe as more dog hair makes its way into our home.

I wasn't always like this.

I remember my first dog, Bingo. I remember loving him as much as I loved my mom and my dad.

I remember being afraid of the drum roll that overtook the sky.

I remember being just like my daughter: the same size, the same fears, the same loves.

I remember when it rained more and the crops thrived. I remember when summer seemed like an eternity and the fireflies at night were endless, just like the tree frogs down the hill. I remember when the days were longer and I didn't need much sleep to function. I remember when I didn't have to worry, or at least I didn't think I had to worry.

Everything is different now.

I worry about not having enough rain rather than worrying the rain will ruin my plans at the pool.

I have nightmares. In the latest, I woke up before the first day of school to find summer was already over. And when I don't get enough sleep, my day is ruined.

But whenever that happens—whenever I start to fret about the future—I remember a very special bottle of Reserva Especial 2001.

In 2008, I fell in love with a wine from La Rioja Alta called Viña Ardanza Reserva 2000.

I waxed poetic about its beauty and grace and about the nostalgia it stirred in me. For twelve months, I enjoyed selling that wine to everyone I knew would appreciate it, be it by the glass with dinner or to take home to the cellar. I loved that wine and shared my love with anyone who was interested.

Every time I sold my last bottle, I would text the distributor to place an order for another case, maybe two. Every time I did this, I would remind myself to buy a bottle to take home and keep as a memory because great wines do not last forever.

You can imagine my surprise and my sadness when my Viña Ardanza came in one day with a different label and a new vintage.

How could I have let this happen? I never saved a single bottle for myself. I let it go. I let it be drunk until it was all gone. I blew it. What was wrong with me that I didn't make sure I had one stashed away as a keepsake?

Then I looked at the new label.

It didn't say *Reserva 2000.* It said *Reserva Especial 2001.*

I looked it up and found that this was the third time the winery had made this bottling in its entire history: 1964, 1973, and, now, 2001.

This was a new bottle, and it was special.

I opened it and took a sip.

It was beautiful. It was regal. It was intense.

It was its own wine.

Change can be scary. It can be sad. It can even overwhelm. But it can also be very, very good.

EPILOGUE

Community and the Future

Twenty years ago, I had a high-profile job in New York City, managing millions of dollars of wine. Now, I'm a small business owner in the town where I was born and raised.

I am a wife, a mother, a public school supporter, and a ball of anxiety.

I wanted to put this journey into words—in fact, I must have written this book a thousand times in my head. But some small voice inside always told me it wasn't safe to do it. Why? Because I'm afraid I'll trivialize the story. Because I'm too afraid to even try to tell it right.

And why is it so important not to trivialize the story? Partly because of the lives that were lost on 9/11 and the need to do them justice. And partly because of everything that's happened since—including the humbling personal growth and community activism I have been able to experience through Tarboro Brewing Company.

Tarboro Brewing Company has easily been the hardest business venture I have ever been involved in. And yet it's also the business that has spurred the most growth in me. It has shaken the dynamics of my family and friendships and with my investors (all of whom are friends as well)—and it has most certainly shaken community dynamics.

When Stephen and I started dreaming up what could go into the space other than a restaurant, we knew telepathically that it was meant for a brewery. I'm fairly certain he thought so because of the space itself, the physicality of the building, but for me, it was different. Something had been missing in Tarboro, and while at the time I believed it was a brewery, I now know it was so much more than that. A community space was exactly what everyone in our county so dearly needed.

As I rebuilt myself during the early years of TBC, I started seeing things differently. One of those things was that more and more couples were working, and when they had time off, they wanted their children with them. We needed a spot for date night that appealed to both adults and children alike.

I also began to see all of the people in my community who were alienated by the menu at On the Square—its prices and its style.

Spaces are vital. Every community needs places they can be together: coworking spaces, family-friendly spaces, places for group activities—places the community can connect, collaborate, encourage and learn from each other.

This realization was a lot to take in all at once, and our brewery space is constantly evolving, changing each and every day as we work to make it more special, accessible, and relevant.

When I think about what has happened in our taproom and our community since 2016, I am humbled and honored by the commitment and the contributions of so many who believed in its importance.

One of our first innovations, which has spawned an unbelievable amount of other community partnerships, is a monthly event called "Cultivating Change: A Community Conversation." This started out as a screening of a short documentary called *Raising Bertie*, which follows three African American boys growing into adulthood in Bertie County, a poor, rural county east of ours. Because we have a large Teach For America (TFA) presence in our county, a lot of educators came to the screening and then asked to be involved in the next steps. This garnered the attention of EducationNC, a nonprofit highlighting public education across the state. Now, they're our sponsors, paying for one beer for every person who comes and actively participates in the conversation. We've covered topics ranging from resilience to clean rivers to nutrition to sexism. I'm not going to lie and tell you it's the most popular event we host, but, for me, it's imperative that we are a space where people can have hard conversations and feel safe at the same time.

Because of the Cultivating Change series, two researchers in our county who are conducting studies on adverse childhood experiences (ACEs) selected our space to host a teen pregnancy workshop based on systems thinking, through Texas A&M University. The five nonprofits that came to the workshop had never visited our brewery, which gave us a chance to show them we're more than just beer brewers—that we are, in fact, a space of education, inclusion, and intentionality.

The more I focused on developing relationships throughout our community, the more positive collaborations seemed to form, completely organically.

We partnered with a local small business owner to use our portico for the outdoor farmers' market two Saturdays a month, from April to October. Then we met a couple in Wake County who were interested in changing careers and invited them to sell her bread at these bi-monthly markets. After a couple of months of success, the couple ended up moving to Tarboro and opening Alimentaire Wholesome Breads bakery. In 2018, they were awarded Entrepreneur of the Year by the NC Rural Center. It was a win for our entire region, and we celebrated with everyone in our community. We still partner with them today: We sell their pretzels in the brewery, and they make butter with our Belgian Dubbel. And one of my favorite beers we have ever made—A Loaf Story—was brewed with their stale bread.

Once Alimentaire opened, another small business popped up: Country Feedback, a vintage store primarily selling records. One of the owners bartends a couple of nights a week at TBC. Her passion for supporting our community emerges in lots of ways, including a collaboration between our businesses and Alimentaire. On a Saturday morning in December, we host a free dress-up cookie-decorating singalong at the brewery, where kids can come in and decorate cookies while singing holiday music. This year, we are incorporating Ace Hardware into the collab to make wreaths with the adults who come in with their children.

We also asked the coffee shop one block down to collaborate by hosting a game night the same night we host trivia so that parents could drink beer and play trivia while their kids played board games and ate ice cream or drank coffee drinks.

One of the TFA corps members, Mr. Stephenson, who not only taught my daughter eighth-grade English but also penned his first book of poetry while sitting at the TBC bar, held his book signing in our taproom and read some of his beautiful poetry aloud. In September of this year, we will release a beer called Hoodie Saison, a collaboration brew we made with Mr. Stephenson (yes, I still call him Mr. Stephenson) to promote his newest book, *Hoodie Season*.

We have bartered with our local merchandiser, a fantastic customer who has designed all of our T-shirts and now even one of our can labels. He feels like he owns the place, and we love that. We want all of our community supporters to feel ownership.

We are the start and end point for a 5K race that benefits our county's cancer support foundation. We also donate beer for the runners over twenty-one who would normally stay and drink a pint or two on their own tab.

When we brew our watermelon beer, if there are watermelons left over, we put them into a plastic wading pool under the portico with a sign that says, "Take a watermelon."

Growing this business has been so much more different than any other experience I have ever known. The team matters on so many levels, and once we invested in a leadership coach who focused on communication, transparency, and accountability, we were able to really build this strong foundation. (Of course, it only took me four years to make that investment.) All three of us on the team moved away, then came back to our hometown to build a life and give back to Tarboro and Rocky Mount, affectionately known as the Twin Counties.

Franklin Winslow, our head brewer and partner, moved to Pennsylvania as a sophomore in high school to attend boarding school at Westtown. He stayed in Pennsylvania for college, then started working at Yards Brewing as their director of quality assurance. Without him, Tarboro Brewing Company would never have been. He is the brewer, the recipe master, the all-things-that-make-great-beer.

Caty Gray Urquhart, the youngest of our small crew, grew up in Tarboro (well, Speed—close enough) and moved to Alexandria, Virginia, for boarding school at Episcopal High School. She stayed away, working as an educator and coach for TFA-Eastern North Carolina before moving back home in 2019. She cold-called me one afternoon in August (similar to the cold call I made to Andrea at Windows in August of 1998) and told me she wanted to work at TBC. When I got back to the office the following day and told the assistant brewer about her call, he immediately made up a two-page list of everything I desperately needed help with. Not humbling at all! Since hiring Caty Gray, I have felt more confident about our path to success than at any other time in the brewery's history. She is the queen of organization, follow-through, and all-around "if I don't know how, I'll find out." Having her on our team is the biggest gift, and in addition to being a phenomenal partner, she has also become a dear friend. I give her the credit for this book actually happening because she has taken on ALL of my duties at some point so that I could bare down and finish this manuscript.

Our business is nowhere near being a full-fledged adult. We have so much to learn, so much to do, so much to give. We have a different economic model than our investors would probably like because what motivates us in our work for our community is not profit but inclusion and actively working to end racism in an organic way.

From allowing couples to hang out with their kids, to a hot dog eating contest, to a wine and design party, to a hospice information session, to giving out candy on Halloween—we have used our brewery to contribute and to educate our neighbors about what we are committed to, not just in beer, but as a supporter of the community. At the end of the day, it's not just about pints, it's about people.

ACKNOWLEDGMENTS

I have spent these last nineteen-and-a-half years writing, erasing, rewriting, and editing the entire journey of the days, months, and years following 9/11. While deeply personal and somewhat painful, my hope in releasing my story is for those who have been devastated by heartbreak to find some form of comfort in this ongoing healing process that if it doesn't kill you will make you stronger and wiser.

I have so many of y'all to thank for pushing me to share the story of coming back home to work and live in the small town that raised me. Each and every word in this book has my community's stamp: my local community, my wine and beer community, and my Windows community. Y'all are my only audience.

And because one of my greatest fears is leaving someone out, I shudder to write these acknowledgments.

However, when it comes to the friends and family department, I literally struck gold, and I consider each and every single one of you God's greatest gifts to me.

To my high school girls who love me even though I gas it up in the grocery store and send y'all texts filled with body parts, I thank you for having loved me since the very beginning.

To my Tarboro, Rocky Mount, and Triangle women who continue to inspire me with fearless leadership and equitable visions for ALL of our children and all people, in general, I wouldn't be who I am without your modeling examples. Thank you for blazing trails and taking names. Strong women for the win!

To my family, I know you have been as nervous and as anxious about this memoir as I have, and I know it's because you work tirelessly to protect me. Y'all have raised me to be who I am, and I give y'all the credit for anything good about me. To say I love you to the moon and back doesn't feel like enough.

To my work families, all of you from Windows to Blue Fin to Borgata to On the Square to TBC, you all are the reason this book exists. Thank you for inspiring me, for pushing me, for tolerating me. I am one fortunate person.